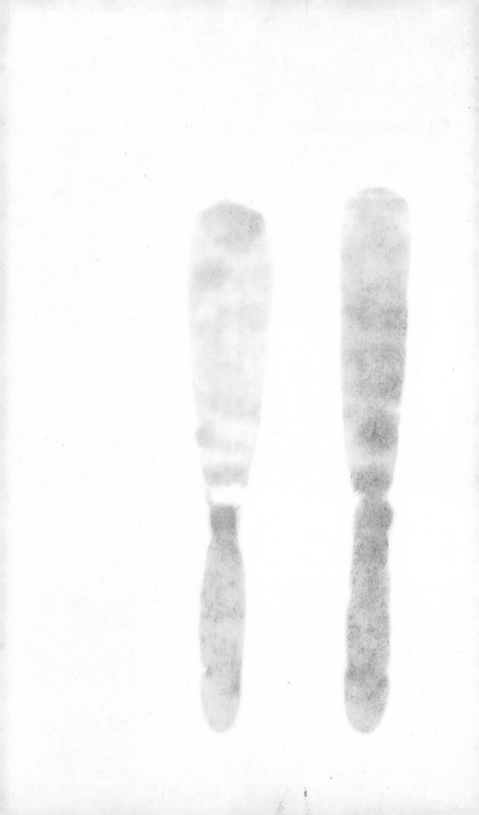

Psychology in Foreign Language Teaching

Psychology in Foreign Language Teaching

STEVEN H. McDONOUGH, M.Sc., MA
Lecturer in Applied Linguistics, University of Essex

London
GEORGE ALLEN & UNWIN
Boston   Sydney

First published in 1981

GEORGE ALLEN & UNWIN LTD
40 Museum Street, London WC1A 1LU

© George Allen & Unwin (Publishers) Ltd, 1981

British Library Cataloguing in Publication Data

McDonough, Steven H
    Psychology in foreign language teaching.
    1. Language and languages – Study and teaching
    2. Educational psychology
    I. Title
    401'.9   P53   80–41626

    ISBN 0–04–418002–0
    ISBN 0–04–418003–9 Pbk

Set in 10 on 11 point Times by Computacomp, Fort William
and printed in Great Britain
by Biddles Ltd, Guildford, Surrey.

Contents

JUN   1983

To Jo

Acknowledgements

I am grateful to the Research Club in Language Learning for permission to reprint the figure on page 68, which originally appeared in the journal *Language Learning*. I should also like to thank Mrs Pat Reader for typing the manuscript so carefully; my colleagues for advice and encouragement; and last but not least many students at the University of Essex who have given me valuable feedback while the book was in preparation.

Chapter 1

Introduction. The Relevance of Psychology

This book is based upon the idea that information about mental processes in learning, understanding and producing language and associated social processes is directly useful for the design, execution and evaluation of language teaching. The science most usually appealed to for such information is psychology, although psychologists do not have a monopoly on it. Whether such information is strictly speaking necessary is a moot point; the claim embodied in the present approach is that teaching based in part on accurate psychological information is less likely to be a hit-and-miss affair, more likely to be conducive to the desired level of achievement, than if such information is either ignored or rejected. In fact most of the major language teaching methods have claimed to incorporate insights from the currently dominant psychological theory. For example, the grammar-translation method appealed to so-called faculty psychology in its emphasis on training the mind; the audio-lingual method incorporated some of the views of behaviouristic learning theory, notably the concept of habit and the law of effect; the cognitive-code method tapped the potentially rich areas of problem-solving.

Naturally, psychological information is not the only kind of information which can be useful. Most authorities would make a case for the utility of linguistic information about the general nature of language and specific descriptions of languages and about the nature of language in use, speech styles, social restrictions on what may be said and how; and for the utility of educational theory in describing how language teaching is supposed to further the general aims of the educational system. Again, most language teaching methods have adhered to some contemporary theoretical models in at least these areas and often several others. The grammar-translation method used parsing into traditional grammatical categories developed for the classical languages; the audio-lingual method used a version of structural linguistics. To the extent that the aims of these two methods were in opposition they subscribed to opposing educational philosophies, the first emphasising analysis, the quickening of intellectual processes, grammar as a mental faculty, and the second emphasising skill and the use of language for definite purposes.

It can be argued that language teaching practice has, in fact, been too heavily influenced by particular theoretical orientations, and that consequently language teachers have been expected to use techniques and types of exercises that appear to be justified in the sense that they are logical applications or extensions of notions derived from the theoretical bases of the method, but which in practice either do not work to the satisfaction of the individual teacher or conversely work too well, resulting in inappropriate language use or errors later in the course when modifications are introduced. A precise and accurate description of some elements of grammar may provide insights as to which items hold the key to the area and what are the most important items and structures to include in the teaching, but it cannot provide a recipe or a rationale for a particular way to teach that part of the language. Similarly, principles of learning and cognitive processes cannot alone provide language teaching exercises. However, the information from these and other sources combined may be properly used to evaluate existing classroom practice and to suggest alternative ways of fulfilling the given goals, and in some cases to suggest other goals which, in the light of this more recent information, may be preferable or more reasonable.

Consequently it is not the aim of this book to propose yet another language teaching method based on the latest research. Rather, theoretical notions and experimental results from psychological research will be reviewed for their relevance to the understanding of how various existing language teaching techniques actually work, and to the evaluation of those techniques in the light of modern conceptions of what 'knowing a language' means; for their power to suggest new techniques; and for gaps that the task of applying research to practical problems might reveal.

Experimental Psychology

Most of the work whose results will be used in the main part of this book employed the methods of empirical or experimental research. There are essentially three reasons for preferring knowledge gained in this way over personal experience, at least when making generalisations and drawing out principles, although the methodology of empirical research is often difficult to follow. For readers who are interested in problems of research methodology, which inevitably involves statistics, there are several easily available texts, for example, Robson (1973). The three reasons referred to above can be stated as three types of error which a science of human behaviour has to avoid in order to conform to the same criteria as other sciences, namely, accuracy, explicitness, availability to public discussion and replicability.

Errors of discrimination

One of the purposes in designing experiments is to be as certain as possible that a particular phenomenon was caused by one event rather than another. Experiments are designed to decide between alternative and competing explanations. For example, some of the most interesting experiments in the psychology of language were designed to decide whether our memory for sentences was itself linguistic in nature, or whether it took some other form such as a visual image. Personal experience alone cannot decide between these alternatives. The answer, incidentally, from that series of experiments was that sentence memory was better regarded as non-linguistic, but not necessarily a visual image of the content of the sentences.

Egocentric error

Another purpose in designing empirical research is to guard against the tendency to believe that what seems to be true of ourselves is true of everybody in a similar situation. This tendency can only be counteracted by observing, under controlled conditions, as many different people as possible. In practice the number does not have to be enormously large, as there are logically defensible statistical techniques which tell the researcher how large a sample of people is needed before any further increase in number brings no increase in reliability. However, it is usually necessary that the sample be representative of the population in ways that are relevant to the point at issue. For example, experienced teachers sometimes assume that, because something has regularly occurred in a certain way in their own classes, it normally occurs this way. Teachers are particularly at risk in this respect because there are normally only few opportunities for them to observe other teachers. An experiment designed to establish some generalisation about this point, whatever it was, would have to look at a large sample of teachers, representative of the profession in terms of personal characteristics such as temperament and training, and representative of the teaching situation in terms of sizes of classes taught, type and level of school, and so on.

Introspection error

The third reason for doing empirical research concerns our limited powers of self-observation. Introspection can be a valuable source of ideas for phenomena to investigate and theories to explain them; but it cannot replace the empirical work because there is no independent way of verifying what one person says of his or her own experience. If I say that I remember the vocabulary of a foreign language as a series of vivid colour images, it may be true, but no one else can ever know exactly what I mean, nor, therefore, know whether it is true. The nineteenth-century school of introspectionist psychology in Germany broke up precisely because no two people could actually agree on their personal experiences. Similarly there are important aspects of mental functioning which are not conscious anyway. While in a conversation we may be conscious of one level of language processing, probably the level of decisions about meaning and our appropriate reaction, we are not conscious of the very important layers of processing which must intervene between meaning and actual grammatically organised utterances. The processes that native speakers go through in this situation are, however, of considerable importance for teaching and learning to speak foreign languages and can only be discovered through experimental research.

However, there is an obvious difficulty here for the consumer anxious to use this empirically gained knowledge for some practical purpose such as designing instructional techniques and materials. The process of paring a phenomenon down to its essentials and removing the confounding influences in the laboratory appears to rob the eventual conclusions of much of their relevance to everyday situations and sometimes produces a reaction of 'So what?' The answer to some theoretical dilemma might have been found, but it is perceived to be abstracted so far away from the complexity and pace of the classroom that it is almost of no use. One should not ignore the fact that this process, and the disappointment which so often follows it in the eyes of the teacher, itself reveals the complexity of the task that learners and teachers of a foreign language are engaged upon and which is worthy of study in its own right.

A learning problem, such as the knotty one of whether it is more efficient to invite students to work out generalisations about, say, sentence structure themselves from a set of examples, or to work out the meaning of a given generalisation on the basis of a set of examples, may be capable of precise formulation in experimental terms. However, in the normal learning situation it will be embedded in all sorts of complications, some of which are relevant and some not. These complications of the real teaching situation are themselves worthy of study, of course, and have been studied to some extent. They might be conveniently grouped under four headings (ignoring the linguistic variables associated with the languages involved).

(a) *Student factors*. Here one might include age, previous learning experience, cognitive style, aptitude, attitudes, motivation, intelligence.
(b) *Teacher factors*. Relevant factors here might be whether the teacher is a native speaker of the foreign language, age, sex, value system, preferred mode of control over the student, attitudes to the language and those who speak it, preferred teaching style, workload, experience.
(c) *Social factors*. Here might be included the cultural and attitudinal differences between the learning group and the native speaker group, the type of social atmosphere in the classroom, the size, composition and cohesion of the classroom group or subgroups, and the type of verbal interaction among teacher and pupils, the mixture of social backgrounds and levels of ability in the classroom.

(d) *Organisational factors.* No two classes are exactly comparable, within or between schools. Contributing to this are variations in organisational type between schools, the relations between staff-room and headmaster, the command structure of the school, the number of pupils demanding certain courses and the supply of teachers, the provision and quality of educational aids, classroom size and decoration.

Bearing in mind this albeit primitive list of complicating factors, it is not surprising that the teacher, who is necessarily aware of them and often doing the job in spite of them, is not impressed by results from the deliberately uncomplicated world of the experimental laboratory or empirical survey. Nevertheless I hope to show in the following pages that information gathered under these conditions is illuminating and useful when properly applied.

The Relation between Psychology and Linguistics

Psychology is only one of several disciplines which study aspects of living things, among the so-called life sciences and the social sciences. It is not the only one to study animal and human behaviour, but in this area discipline boundaries are impossible to draw with any consistency. However, for many years neither psychologists nor linguists saw much relevance for their work in each other's fields and methods of study. Psychologists were thought to study behaviour, mainly at a simple level, and linguists sought methods of describing languages and the history of languages. There was some cross-fertilisation of ideas in the work of Bloomfield (1933), who noted the significance of some versions of the habit formation theory of learning for his ideas of structural grammar. However, linguists working since the Second World War have been increasingly compelled to view their work on unravelling the enormous complexity of any human language, as compared to an animal communication system, as holding great significance for theories of the nature of mind, of cognitive processes in general, and even for the genetic endowment which shapes our intellectual maturation. Chomsky (1965) in a famous passage claimed that linguistics was indeed a branch of cognitive psychology. This claim was a cause of considerable controversy both among linguists and between linguists and many psychologists, particularly those of the behaviourist school. Nevertheless, many researchers were attracted by the possibility of working on language problems with the benefit of both the experimental and statistical expertise of the psychological laboratory and the conceptual richness and mathematical elaboration of Chomskyan linguistics. Psycholinguistics, as the new field came to be called, has had a somewhat chequered career, due partly to the inherent complexities of the subject and partly to the rather fundamental philosophical differences between many psychologists and linguists over aims and methods of inquiry. These have centred on the validity of using data from real people performing linguistic tasks to infer theoretically significant generalisations about the nature of language and linguistic processes rather than deducing both from the right set of axioms. This difference of approach is related to the very old debate between philosophical empiricists and rationalists. Nevertheless it has generated a considerable amount of investigation into the comprehension, production and acquisition of language and these topics will be examined in Chapters 4 and 7 for their usefulness in the foreign language situation.

A Linking Science

In the light of the considerations already mentioned it is clear that some framework is needed for discussing applications of basic research, that is, research conducted for the purpose of building theories, to the practical situation of language learning and teaching, with the aim of improving the efficiency of language instruction. The American psychologist R. Glaser (1976) has suggested four necessary components of such a framework, which he calls a 'science of the design of instruction'. I shall add a fifth, which he subsumes into a wider category. The five components are these:

(1) *Analysis of the conditions that can be manipulated to change a novice into an expert*

Glaser intends by this an examination of the instructional techniques available and suggested in terms of known parameters of learning. That is to say, what effect does a particular training procedure have and what part of the learning process is affected?

(2) *Analysis of competent performance*

What does speaking and understanding a foreign language actually involve? How do we make sense of the stream of sounds? What relationship do these processes have to our performance in the native language? What, exactly, does it mean to be an expert non-native speaker?

(3) *Analysis of the development of competent performance*

Glaser subsumes this component under (1), but I have given it special prominence. The reason is that (1) concentrates, quite rightly, on instructional techniques and their effects but there should also be equal concern for the gradual development of autonomy of the learning process as the expertise develops. This is true of any skill, but is particularly important in language learning, which may continue over a period of years and involve successive reorganisation by the learner of material he has learned and skills he has acquired to take account of new demands and new material. This contribution by the learner requires and repays careful study.

(4) *Analysis of the initial state of the learner*

Before suggesting how educational aims may be implemented we need a description of where the novice is starting from. This is particularly important in language learning, in contrast to other subjects and skills, as he invariably has at least spoken proficiency in his native language, a proficiency which he might never reach in the new language to be learnt. This raises all sorts of interesting and difficult problems. As well as this, most language learners bring to the situation differences of motivation and aptitude, both in kind and degree, as mentioned under 'student factors' above.

(5) *Evaluation of the process and product of learning*

Educational assessment is a very difficult area; it is mostly concerned with assessment of achievement or attainment, also with diagnosis of learning problems and to some extent, and rather controversially, with prediction. But it is also necessary to develop realistic criteria for evaluating the instructional and learning processes, not only to know if they were successful, but also to know how they interrelated with other parts of the total experience. For example, one might ask what general improvement in reading skill can be expected from such and such an exercise (such as questions after the passage) besides the attainment of comprehension of that particular passage; and what learning difficulties are being created for a future stage by treating this grammar point now in this particular way.

The Organisation of This Book

In this book we begin with a discussion of the very influential school of psychology loosely known as associationism or behaviourism, of the types of analyses of the above problems which can be derived from their work, and we illustrate this by reference to some well-known language teaching techniques and syllabus designs. We then move to the rather different analyses and solutions derived from work which has emphasised the flow of information and skill learning. Chapter 4 examines some of the more important results from recent psycholinguistic research on language comprehension and production. Chapter 5 examines the concept of memory and the vexed question of how learners organise what they have learned in order not to forget it and also be able to use it on demand. Next, in Chapter 6, we look at social-psychological concerns, both in the wider context of social motivation and the narrower one of the classroom and the dynamics of small learning groups. After these chapters describing implications from general psychology there follow two specifically about language learners: Chapter 7, about the learning of the native tongue and to what extent foreign language teachers need take notice of the increasing amount of knowledge in this field; Chapter 8 is concerned with second language learners and some of the main results and implications of direct studies of the development of second language expertise. We end with two chapters about individual differences: Chapter 9 concerns individual traits that are associated with attainment and different ways, or strategies, of learning. Chapter 10 discusses several approaches to motivation in the foreign language context.

Although each chapter contains material which is of relevance to each of the five types of analysis discussed above, each chapter may be seen as contributing primarily to one or other of the components. Chapters 2 and 3 are mainly concerned with the analysis of the conditions that can be manipulated and Chapter 6 also contains relevant material. Chapters 4 and 5, and parts of Chapter 6, mainly discuss the analysis of competent performance. Chapters 7 and 8 look at the analysis of the development of competence, and Chapters 9 and 10 examine aspects of the initial state of the learner and how that state may be affected by the learning experience. All of the chapters contain material which is relevant to the assessment of the process of instruction. Each chapter opens with questions arising out of the practice of language teaching and closes with discussion of actual examples of teaching or learning activities.

Finally, there are two groups of words which persistently cause confusion. The first group is 'learning' and 'acquisition'. The term 'acquisition' was originally introduced into discussions of children and their native language in order to avoid the behaviourist, learning theory associations of the word 'learning'. In the last ten years or so, discussants of second language learning have also wished to be free of such a hidden allegiance and have also used the term 'acquisition' without, however, necessarily intending to mean that the processes of first and second language acquisition are the same, although this has been one of the points under examination. In this book the term 'learning' will be used, but without thereby committing the author to any particular theoretical position.

The second confusing group is the set of terms to denote non-native languages. First language (L_1) will mean native language (contrary to the usage in many schools, where it means first foreign language), and languages learnt subsequently will be given ordinal numbers chronologically, that is, second language (L_2), or third language (L_3). Unless specified, the term 'second language' is not to be thought of as bearing a distinction from 'foreign language'.

The reason for this neutral approach is simply that the bases of the various distinctions commonly made in both these groups of words form the subject matter of the book.

In what follows, the language of example will be mainly English, and the major concern will be the learning of English as a second language, but the principles discussed may be regarded as relevant to the teaching and learning of any language.

Chapter 2

Behaviourism

This chapter is concerned with the ideas of a particularly influential school of psychology who pioneered the use of controlled observation to discover laws of behaviour. In distinguishing behaviourism from alternative schools, such as the functionalism of the early 1920s and the Gestaltism of the 1930s, there is a danger that the differences between the schools can be overemphasised at the expense of the differences within them. For example, later in this chapter we shall see how several of the major criticisms of behaviourist thought attributed to cognitive psychologists actually arose within the behaviourist school in discussion of animal behaviour. However, although there never was a monolithic body of coherent and articulated behaviourist theory with no internal tensions, there was broad agreement on certain principles, particularly of method and subject matter.

Similarly, cognitive psychologists do not all adhere to a body of theory which is well articulated and in opposition to the behaviourist one. Rather, the argument about what exactly are the data, descriptions, experimental tasks and theories which are most useful, revealing, and general for explaining human behaviour has progressed slowly and with a great deal of controversy. A good account of this controversy as it relates to the analysis of behaviour can be found in D. E. Broadbent (1961).

Language teachers have often queried the relative usefulness in class of techniques such as repetition, memorisation, imitation, explanation, conscious application of rules, slotting different vocabulary items into patterns, comprehension questions, reading aloud, delaying reading until a stage of oral-aural command is reached, and many others. Language teaching methods have usually taken a selection of these techniques and grouped them under some integrating principle which is supposed to give a purpose and a role for the techniques in relation to the aims of the course and the other techniques. In claiming validity for the particular conception of language or language learning that acts as this integrating principle, the authors quote authorities in linguistics and psychology who support their contentions. J. B. Carroll, writing in 1966, warned that the then currently dominant language teaching methods were not in fact based on contemporary psychological work but used, loosely and selectively, older concepts:

> Let me point out that neither the audiolingual habit theory nor the cognitive code learning theory is closely linked to any contemporary psychological theory of learning. The audiolingual habit theory has a vague resemblance to an early version of a Thorndikean association theory, while the cognitive code learning theory is reminiscent of certain contemporary gestaltist movements in psychology which emphasise the importance of perceiving the structure of what is to be learned, without really relying on such movements. (Carroll, 1966, p. 104)

In this and the following chapter we look at the main features of the behaviourist and the cognitivist schools in order to see what the psychological bases of the claims of audio-lingual and other language teaching theories are and what new light has been shed on those claims by more recent advances in theory and experiment. There is a double purpose here: to discover the psychological justifications for designing language teaching in certain ways and to assess the adequacy of those justifications in the light of other information.

Central Tenets of Associationism

Learning is controlled by the consequences of behaviour
E. L. Thorndike was the first behaviourist to research the idea that learning consisted of the establishment of associations between particular pieces of behaviour and the consequences of that behaviour. The evidence for the establishment of such associations he took to be the increased probability that in a similar set of circumstances similar behaviour would be produced. Thus a cat will learn to contrive its escape from a box if the first act of escaping is rewarded immediately; in the situation a second time it will do again whatever it was doing just before it got the reward. Thus an action which may originally have been random or accidental, like brushing against some part of the box, will be repeated if it was followed previously by reward. Thorndike described this by saying that an associative bond had been set by the closeness in time of the particular action and the reward. In his terminology, the bond would be 'stamped in' by repetition of the action and its consequence. He also argued that the bond would be 'stamped out', that is, forgotten or unlearned, if the action were followed by a painful experience, which might be like punishment.

This principle of learning by consequences or payoff has had a long career. It is, of course, nicely commonsensical that actions followed by reward tend to be repeated. The wide use of this principle in audio-lingual language teaching is what Carroll is referring to above. For example, teachers are encouraged to show approval for each and every correct performance by their pupils, and every drill is designed so that the possibility of making mistakes is minimised, engineering success for the pupils. What food was for the cat, success is for the pupils.

Unfortunately for this principle, many earlier behaviourists attempted to make it into the only, or most fundamental, principle. Thorndike called it the law of effect. However, it soon became obvious that there were several kinds of behaviour which people wanted to call learning because they seemed to lead to a relatively permanent change, but which were established without reward. In the 1930s there was considerable discussion about latent, or incidental, learning and whether it could be described within the terms of the law of effect. In a typical latent learning experiment the performance of rats which were new to a maze was compared to that of some which had seen the maze before, but without receiving reward. The second group usually performed better. Common sense is again satisfied, and most of us would say the second group had learned something of the layout of the maze. But this cannot be predicted on any simple version of the law of effect; they did not receive any reward for learning the layout at the time. Modern ethologists would explain this rather in terms of the animals' natural exploratory behaviour: a cat, for example, will explore every avenue left open for it in a new house.

Despite this and other embarrassments for the law of effect, which had appeared in the home ground of animal experimentation, the educational world of the 1950s still placed considerable trust in the idea of learning by consequences.

Measurement of observables

The behaviourist psychologists of the 1930s believed in a philosophy of science which constrained them only to take account of what they could see or record in behaviour and freed them from the desire to consider imperceptible 'mental events'. This was variously adhered to. Skinner, for example, refused to consider any theoretical symbolisation of unobserved events and maintained that behaviour was adequately described simply by a direct relationship between responses and features of the reward such as frequency, amount, delay, and so on. Hull argued that most learning was too complex to be accounted for by such simple functions, and that one had to postulate 'intervening variables' between stimulus, response, and reward, which could not be observed, only inferred from behaviour. The problem that arises is how to make and validate the inferences. Hull and his followers argued that there were several kinds of internal responses, for example, 'fractional anticipatory goal responses' (r_g) or 'mediating responses' (r_m), which were learned, and fitted the same laws as the observed, external responses. For example, a rat's recognising the right path at the beginning of a learnt maze was described in terms of a series of internal responses leading, via a hierarchy of habits, to the external response of actually making the turn. This way there was no need to have recourse to mentalist and vague terms such as 'choice or thought', either for animal or human behaviour.

Such attitudes, involving either complete rejection of internal events or very limited incorporation of them as mini-versions of the overt behaviour, were also consonant with the ideas of the structural linguists, who were more concerned with the description of the sound system and the grammatical system of languages than with problems of meaning and how meanings are expressed in utterances. (See, for example, the work of Bloomfield (1933) or Fries (1952) and the commentary by Dinneen (1967, ch. 9.)) Consequently it is not surprising that language teaching owing theoretical allegiance to these schools of thought insisted on the primacy of sound and structural patterns and largely ignored, or considered easily postponable, the expansion of the students' vocabulary or the students' natural desire to express an opinion of his own.

However, even in animal experimentation it soon became obvious that the simple models excluding internal events were just too simple and that some viable theoretical constructs were needed. In other words, behaviour itself is too complex to be described solely in its own, external, terms, even in lower animals; some way of describing the knowledge that underlies it is also needed. 'Fractional anticipatory goal responses' were attempts at describing knowledge by assuming it was just internalised behaviour. However, it was shown many years ago, again with rats, that animals trained to run a maze would be able to swim the maze, so the map of the maze they had learned must have been relatively abstract, not simply a pattern of movements.

Contiguity

According to Thorndike, Watson, Hull, and to some extent Skinner, the only link between a response and its reward, or the association between stimulus and response and the reward, was time. Two repeated events would become associated if they were close enough in time. This principle is the basis of all exhortations, in educational settings, to give praise immediately, or to arrange the drills and exercises so that the student experiences success frequently and is told about that success immediately. Skinner developed this principle to include altering the rate of reward so as to get maximum learning performance. However, the contiguity principle is not always valid even in the limited intellectual world of the rat. Rats which are made to run a maze twice, once for food and once for water, will remember the position of the water better, the further away it was from the food (Deutsch, 1956, described in Broadbent, 1961).

So, reward does not have to follow immediately; two things widely separated in time may be associated; and much learning can take place without reward. Of course, these statements sound like common sense, but when so much educational practice has been based on their denial it is instructive to look at the counter-evidence arising from the rat laboratory.

Response strength

The amount of learning was measured by the probability that a particular response would be emitted. Thus learning was defined in terms reminiscent of electric lights or buckets of water: the response glowing brightest or containing the most water was the strongest. The concept of strength is also behind the Skinnerian use of the term 'reinforcement' to cover rewards and other actions which strengthen the response. This strength view is the basis for the audio-lingual theorists' insistence that new structures should first be drilled to an automatic stage before being contrasted with others or used in dialogue or free conversation. It is also basic to the view summarised by Politzer in this famous quotation: 'Language is "behaviour" and ... behaviour can be learned only by inducing the student to "behave" ', which is taken by Rivers (1964) as the starting point of one of her most important chapters.

Leaving aside for the moment the question of whether language is behaviour and what that might mean, we have to question whether it is only behaviour we want the students to learn, or both skilled behaviour and underlying knowledge. The conception of learning as increasing response strength conflates the two aspects: no distinction is made between increasing frequency of response and increasing complexity or structure of response. We have already seen how attempts to describe internal events in terms of external behaviour foundered, even with rats; the complexity of human behaviour, especially of language, demands a quite different and infinitely richer set of concepts. The audio-lingual methodologists insisted that one should 'Teach the language, and not about the language' (Moulton, 1961); and, in so far as they were concerned about reducing the amount of class time devoted to explanations of grammatical structure and about increasing the proportion of pupil talk in the foreign language, they were sensible. However, complexity of language is such that one cannot say that a person knows a language when certain behavioural responses have been strengthened; rather, knowing a language implies knowledge of complex structures and procedures which is a necessary prerequisite of practical performance.

Generalisation

The behaviourists argued that there was a gradient in the law of effect. Reward strengthened the response it followed; but it also strengthened responses to other stimuli in proportion to their degree of similarity to the original stimulus. Thorndike tried to capture this gradient in his principle of transfer of training, the law of identical elements. Learning would be transferred in proportion to the number of identical elements in the various stimuli. Thus different stimuli would evoke the same response, but the strength of the response in each case would depend on the relative number of identical elements in the original stimulus and in the new one. This was strictly stimulus generalisation; a similar principle was held to govern the effect of reward to one response on other possible similar responses, namely, response generalisation. Skinner held a similar view, using the term 'induction'.

The importance of this phenomenon, and the extension of S–R theory it made necessary, was that it offered an objective account of how analogies are formed without resorting to speculative and mentalistic notions. It was this principle that gave the main impetus to the audio-lingual pattern drill. A set of phrases or sentences is given, to which the learner has to make the same response, or on which he has to perform the same manipulation. The simplest form is the substitution table:

How many questions can you ask?

	a car		big		a scooter	
Is	a horse	as	heavy	as		?
	a train		expensive		an aeroplane	
			safe			

(Broughton, 1968, Vol. I, p. 42)

As long as the student follows the instruction to choose one word from each division in the given order, success in making grammatically correct questions is guaranteed. However, ultimately the only overt connections the resulting sentences have with each other is the repeated frame

$$Is \text{——} as \text{——} as \text{——}?$$

and the fact that they were rewarded, either intrinsically by success, or extrinsically by approval:

> Is a horse as heavy as an aeroplane?   Good.
> Is a train as safe as a scooter?   Good.

The drill is designed to induce in the student the generalisation that words can be joined together like this for a certain purpose (that of comparison), and to make this unthinking and automatic. All the twenty-four possible sentences form a set linked by analogy and sentences using different words can be formed on this basis. There is, however, nothing in the drill itself to indicate to the student what sort of words can fit in the various slots: to indicate to him that

> Is a loud as house as a blue?

is not grammatical or meaningful. He is expected to induce a principle of similarity in the analogy, namely, that the divisions indicate form-classes, viz., nouns, adjectives, nouns. This most students do, either from direct inspection of the meaning or from mother-tongue equivalents. The important point here, however, is that this kind of knowledge does not come from the gradient of generalisation, but from additional sources.

Chaining and shaping

If an animal is trained to respond with one movement and then is no longer rewarded for that alone but only when it is followed by a second movement, the two responses may be said to be chained together. Hence Skinner was able to teach pigeons to follow rather complicated routines, like dancing a figure of eight or playing ping-pong. Each successive link in the chain was 'shaped', that is to say, when the animal made even a slight movement in the required direction some reward would be given, and the frequency and intensity of that movement would increase. For the pigeon dancing a figure of eight, right turns would be rewarded, then only right turns followed by a left turn of the head, then only right turns followed by a left turn of the body, then only right turns followed by left turns followed by walking straight, and so on. This chain of associations was seen as a possible model for complex human activities like language, a question we take up below.

It has sometimes been argued that teaching foreign language pronunciation can be done by 'shaping by successive approximation'. The student is encouraged to produce repetitively a suitable sound in his own language and is rewarded each time there is a phonetic variation in the direction of the foreign language sound until gradually only productions of the new sound are rewarded. While this may have some success, it is more likely that teachers who claim to use it in fact model the new sound for the student, thus adding an element of mimicry which is not present in the original conception of behaviour shaping and rather changes the situation. In fact, pure reward-controlled shaping would be very difficult for training speech sounds, as there are quite complex rules governing their perceptibility and distinctness which have to be set aside if the phonological system of the new language is approached through that of the old.

What Picture of Language did these Ideas imply?

There have been several attempts to develop a theory of language structure on associationist lines. Mowrer (1954), Osgood (1963) and Skinner (1957) are the best-known. Roughly speaking, they all worked on the idea that different parts of sentences were conditioned upon or associated with the other parts because the conjunction of those bits of sentences had been rewarded in the past. Put crudely, the four elements of

Peter kicked the bucket

were uttered in that order because that pattern (not necessarily those words, because of the principle of generalisation) had been rewarded in the past and, further, because that pattern is an associative chain, each element directly dependent on the previous one.

The best-known of these associationist accounts of language is that of Skinner (1957), who claimed it was a functional account, and one reason why it is so well known is that Chomsky chose to review it from the perspective of modern linguistics. Among the points he chose to criticise were the following:

Language is stimulus-bound

Chomsky ridiculed Skinner for claiming that utterances can be seen as learned responses to stimuli. We do not say things to people because of past reward. On the other hand, as we shall see when considering social psychology, language is not entirely stimulus-free; a large proportion of what we say depends on features of the situation, particularly the social situation, and the knowledge each conversation partner attributes to the other. However, no S–R mechanism can represent these complexities.

Language structure can be explained in terms of reinforcement, generalisation, strength, contiguity

Chomsky argued that these terms could probably be given precise meaning in the animal laboratory, but were useless when extrapolated to the complexities of language. Either they could only explain trivial issues – such as a child only getting what he wanted when he said 'Please' – or they were vacuous, that is, empty of meaning outside the original animal laboratory context. We have already seen how even in that context these concepts had been challenged by the 1950s. The behaviourist attempts to explain language structure in terms of these concepts were dismissed by Chomsky as translations of traditional grammar which added nothing and indeed merely further confused the issue because of the vacuity of the terms. We have already seen that the notion of generalisation of response by transfer of identical elements is inadequate to explain the learning of the normal order of form-classes in simple sentence frames. This point about learning the grammatical order of words by contextual generalisation was the focus of a famous debate between Braine and Bever, Fodor and Weksel.

Language structure is an associative chain

Chomsky was able to prove that chain structures are not possible grammars for language. An example will suffice to demonstrate this. In

The man who sang was a singer

was is more closely related to *man* than to *sang*, but in an associative chain, each successive link is only related directly to the previous one. Language is thus hierarchically ordered – traditional grammarians would have said that *who sang* is a clause inserted into the main clause to modify *the man*. In fact, Osgood's associative model claims to represent this hierarchy, but can only do so by asking us to believe that internal mediating responses can act as internal stimuli for other internal responses at a more abstract level.

Language does not imply knowledge, only performance

We have already seen that behaviourists other than Skinner were grappling with the problem of how to represent events inside the skull: that is, with describing knowledge and decisions that their results showed had to be ascribed even to their lowly rats. Chomsky argued strongly that language could not be understood without recourse to the concept of underlying knowledge. Ambiguous sentences demonstrate this:

Visiting relatives can be a nuisance.

The difference between the two interpretations of this is not marked in the superficial structure. He further made the point that inferring the knowledge from behaviour, from examples of everyday speech, was doomed to failure. This opinion, which revealed the huge philosophical gap between the representatives of the two disciplines, has been hotly debated ever since between and within the disciplines.

Educational Uses of Behaviourist Ideas

Chomsky's review of Skinner's book seemed to mark the end of simplistic extrapolation from animal learning to complex human functioning, especially language. However, in educational circles behaviourist principles continued to be popular, and one reason for this was the advent of programmed instruction. Embodied in programmed instruction (PI) were many of the principles mentioned earlier, extrapolated to an educational context. There is no doubt they were intended as a radical attack on the rather stultifying educational procedures of the late 1940s and 50s, with rule-learning, meaningless parroting, translation, learning by heart, punitive attitudes, and the concomitant lack of well thought out educational objectives. The following could be regarded as the most important features of PI.

(1) *Objectives must be stated precisely and fully*   Just as one cannot train a pigeon to dance a figure of eight without knowing what 8 looks like, so one cannot teach a language without deciding exactly what to teach and why. However, this desirable quality is not the property only of behaviourist teaching; it is justifiable on other grounds as well.

(2) *The material to be learned is divided into very small steps*   This is to ensure maximum success, or rather a minimum error rate, and the

steps are determined by repeated trials with sample customers. At least this is the method in a linear programme, in which the student's response is productive – he produces an answer in accordance with the principle of response strength. In another type of programme, the branching type, the student has to recognise the correct answer out of a set of alternatives. If his choice is incorrect he is directed to further examples which should clear up the point. Because a linear programme has to be very carefully constructed to ensure that the response produced by the student is in fact the one required it has been remarked that ultimately each learner needs his own programme. A branching programme can cater for a wider range of learning by substituting recognition for active production of the response; such a programme cannot be successful if a majority of students follow side branches for most of the time. This feature of low error rate was a welcome trend in schools where for a long time a punitive attitude to learning had been the tradition: now there was apparently a scientific justification for teaching in which the pupils achieved rapid and continuing success, with the motivational benefits which that should entail. Many language teaching courses that were not programmed in the strict sense adopted this principle of error avoidance.

(3) *Programmes are individually paced* Thus the aim is to finish the programme, not to do so within a time set for the group. In this way individual differences in ability and intelligence can be ignored: since the step size is empirically determined, any subject matter can in principle be learnt by anybody, regardless of such differences, given time. Organisationally, this promised to be the most disruptive feature, since normal timetabling of classes would be impossible. Furthermore, completion of the programme implied success within it, and so separate end-of-course assessment was not necessary, and the tensions associated with examinations could be replaced by enjoyment and satisfaction all round.

Not surprisingly, such heady promises or ideals are not so easily put into practice. With languages, the sheer quantity of material makes this small-step drip-feed method unrealistic. Also, difficult linguistic problems arise out of the complexity of the grammatical system; we have already seen that the associative chain is too simple for modelling language structure. Finally, there is a paradox in using an individual self-instructional method, even assuming the problems of reducing language structure to small steps have been overcome, for a skill which is essentially communicative. Nowadays programmed self-instructional materials are normally only used as remedial back-up work for students in difficulties over a particular point.

Analysis of some Behaviourist Techniques

A continuing theme in this chapter has been the adequacy of the associationist account of learning. In examining some of the language teaching techniques derived from it, we should look for both the behaviourist features and other elements that may explain how the technique works (or fails to work). We are not primarily concerned with whether it is good language teaching as this can only be determined in relation to the aims of a particular course. Here is a sample laboratory drill, which could easily be adapted for round-the-class drilling or individual and choral response work.

A picture of a living room is provided

Example: [all on tape]
(Model Teacher) *Ask if the table is in the room.*

(Model Pupil) *Is the table in the room?*

(Model Teacher) *Is the table in the room?*

(Model Pupil) *Is the table in the room?*

Now you do these:
Tape: *Ask if the TV is in the room.*

Pupil: ——

Tape: *Is the TV in the room?*

Pupil: ——

Tape: *Yes. Ask if the clock is in the room.*

Pupil: ——

Tape: *Is the clock in the room?*

Pupil: ——

Tape: *Yes. Ask if the cat is in the room.*

Pupil: ——

Tape: *Is the cat in the room?*

Pupil: ——

[and so on]

The first point to note is that the students are required to make an active response but that it is modelled fully for them. They are not asked to produce something which can be shaped up into the desired behaviour, but a full response from the beginning. Shaping would be possible if the picture was given with the instruction 'Ask some questions about it like this', but shaping is not in fact used here. Also, the model is supposed to be clear. In fact, many students do not understand that they are supposed to make an active and creative response but prefer to wait until they can just repeat the taped response. This is a local danger with this way of giving the instruction.

Secondly, note that this drill is in four phases:

(1) stimulus
(2) active response
(3) model response
(4) repetition.

The active response, on the basis of the taped example, could be produced either by rearrangement of the elements according to some rule, or by rote. The method does not distinguish between these two options open to students. The model response is designed to act as a reward only in the case where the exercise is easy enough for the student to get it nearly right first time, but of course in more difficult exercises the student will not perceive it as a reward. The student has to compare his answer with the one supplied and is then given a further opportunity to practise. Student self-evaluation is implicit in all behavioural techniques, but there is no explanation in behaviourist theory as to how it can happen. One could imagine, anthropomorphically, that the pigeon doing its dance has to compare the movements which bring reward with those that do not in order to maximise reward. Although this might be seen as attributing too much cerebration to the bird, some such evaluation of outcomes has to be built into a goal-directed device. The students in the booths have to evaluate their own responses (usually, of course, with the dubious aid of the wire-tapping teacher), but behaviourist theory is inadequate for telling us how they do it or how best to help them.

Thirdly, we can ask what is being learned here. Essentially each item brings a new word to put into the pattern *Is the —— in the room?* This can be done without attention to either the structure of the question or that of the instruction. Indeed, the principle of automaticity of response requires that there be no such attention. Such drills Dakin (1973) claimed led to a strange language-like performance he termed 'structure speech', which was correct drill performance, but not language. Since the whole drill can be performed correctly without attention to the ostensible aim of the drill, namely, *yes/no* question formation, while attention is diverted to comparison of the response and its intonation with the model, there is an important sense in which the student is not relating his response to the instruction *Ask* ... and therefore is not practising question formation at all.

Fourthly, it is probably significant that even courses that subscribe to behaviourist tenets relegate this type of drill to follow-up work in the laboratory. This is most likely to be used as practice, not presentation.

Nevertheless, techniques of round-the-class and down-the-rows rapid–fire drilling are used as presentation methods, and where this is so, many of the same comments apply. E. Rothkopf (1970) referred to this form of teaching as 'the calculus of practice'.

Finally in this chapter we look at the question of sequencing the language material. There are many ways of doing this; and many problems in grading material for presentation and exploitation. Here we are concerned with whether a language syllabus can be considered to be an associative chain. In the following, a sequence of grammatical items is followed lesson by lesson. The transition from lesson to lesson is intended to enable material in one lesson to prepare the ground for the next; and conversely for material in the next to appear to grow out of the previous one. Opportunities for error are to be avoided. We take up the story well into the first year, when the students already know demonstratives, copula *is/are*, pronouns, *can*, and several other items, each of which has been drilled to exhaustion.

Lesson (l)	has drilled copula and adjective combinations: *She is happy*
Lesson (m)	introduces the *-ing* form: *She is driving a car*
Lesson (n)	reintroduces existential *there*: *There is a man standing near the car*
Lesson (o)	distinguishes between mass and count nouns: *There are some oranges and some cheese on the table*
Lesson (p)	introduces the verbs *like* and *want*: *I like oranges but not cheese*
Lesson (q)	reintroduces *don't*, previously known in negative imperatives: *I don't like cheese*
Lesson (r)	introduces verbs with stative meaning: *I don't come from Newcastle*
Lesson (s)	introduces adverbs of habit and thus the present simple tense; or rather, present tense in simple aspect: *I usually come at six o'clock*

(This is an invented example based on several behaviourist/structuralist courses)

Each step in this sequence uses information presented in the previous one; the student can rightfully feel a sense of progress. Three points are important about this syllabus.

First, each step seems to be indeed a link in a chain, and this could be represented graphically as in Figure 2.1. Of course, this can only be regarded as analogous to the chain of turns framing the pigeons' dance, not as identical in principle; the items are so much more complicated, and the

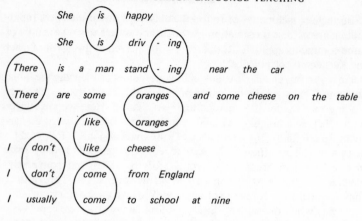

Figure 2.1 *A chainlike sequence in a syllabus.*

succeeding items are not shaped up from randomly emitted movements, but planned in advance in strict fashion.

Secondly, the language items are chosen so as to avoid error opportunities. Having drilled the *-ing* form, it is then dropped from use while the run-up to the present simple is progressing; eventually, of course, they will be drilled contrastively:

> *Today I am going to school on the bus.*
>
> *Usually I go to school on foot.*

(Note that in this contrastive drill choice of aspect is signalled unambiguously by the first word; another analogy with the sentence as a conditioning device). The first non-copula verbs introduced, with *don't*, are precisely ones which are very rarely used in the continuous form, so there is little likelihood that material in the lessons will encourage the students to say 'I am liking oranges', although this cannot be totally prevented.

Thirdly, it will be noticed that several times structures that have been introduced and used as links in the chain are actually slightly contorted for the purpose of pedagogy: for example, *happy* and *driving* are equated distributionally by being allowed to follow the copula, but belong to different grammatical form classes; as a corollary, *is* is used as a copula and as an auxiliary in the two lessons, but this difference is not brought to the attention of the students. When overlearnt, strong responding is the aim, such differences are ignored. Naturally, in many cases, this roughshod riding over grammatical distinctions may lead to errors rather late in the course. The use of *come* in two distinct senses, as in *come from* 'be a native of' and as in *come to* 'arrive', could prove to be just such a problem, requiring awkward unlearning later.

Inspection of this syllabus fragment has demonstrated how language material may be exposed to students in ways analogous to associationist animal training, but that those concepts are not really adequate to describe the learning processes of the students, and that forcing language material into these techniques distorts the material and misrepresents it to the students.

Chapter 3

Information-Processing Approaches

In the quotation in the last chapter Carroll (1966) argued that whereas at that time language teaching approaches might be dichotomised into two types and each of those rested on different psychological backgrounds neither of them incorporated recent findings or explicit modern theories in any kind of detailed and systematic fashion.

There could be many reasons for this apparent lack of communication between various areas of pure research and course writers or classroom practitioners; one is probably the inability of any school or focus of research to shed light on or explain more than a restricted part of the total process of learning a foreign language in school. In the previous chapter, some behaviourist drills were analysed in terms of generalisation; however, it is more than likely that in actual classrooms teachers use other techniques of presentation to get the students to understand the grammatical principle involved. These other techniques are probably derived from non-behaviourist psychology, if they owe anything to psychology at all. In a later paper Carroll (1971) referred to this tendency towards eclecticism, apparently disavowing his earlier dichotomy by proposing a 'cognitive habit formation theory'.

It is therefore not surprising that language teaching has also borrowed from psychology some of the basic insights into the processes of understanding and concept formation and has often used these side by side with behaviourist training techniques, despite the inherent conflicts and contradictions entailed thereby at a theoretical level.

Thus recourse has often been had to other traditions in psychology: those concerned with specifying the nature of inferred unobservable events, like the structure of perception and cognition, and the intake, selection, categorisation, storage and retrieval of information. As we shall see, models of these processes have usually been quite different from the simple strength analogies used by learning theorists.

Another reason to look at different psychological models is the apparent inability of behaviourism to explain in sufficient detail what students do when they are faced with an exercise ostensibly based on it. Hosenfeld (1976) asked pupils to tell her what they actually did while performing some traditional classroom language drills. She had them introspect and report their own strategies for getting the answers right. It became obvious that the students were reducing the mechanical transformation drills to their barest essentials and although the answers were then correct the procedures being practised were not very useful. For example, one student described her own performance of a simple mechanical drill in French, replacing an object noun phrase by a pronoun in front of the verb (*Ils ont perdu les bérets verts = Ils les ont perdus*), in the following way:

> On number two [*Elle a vendu la maison*] I look at *la*, put 'l' in front of *a* and add 'e' to *vendu*. On three [*J'ai regardé les beaux tableaux*] I look at *les*; *beaux* is masculine; otherwise it would be *belles*, and I put 'les' in front of the verb ... and add 's' to *regardé*. I don't pay any attention to what the sentence is saying ... I just look for the *le*, *la*, *les*, put it in front of the verb, and if it's *les* I look at the adjective a little bit. (Hosenfeld, 1976, p. 122)

It is obvious that a behaviourist account of learning says virtually nothing about the complex reasoning process used by this student and so can offer little help to the teacher who wishes to nurture it and perhaps redirect it. Nevertheless, one should remember that the growing despondency about the utility of this sort of practice was one of the factors that led to the adoption of behaviourist methods as a replacement rather than an improvement in the first place, and so one must be careful in evaluating this student's report. Two things stand out clearly; first, she does not make reference to the meaning of the sentence and she is not required to and secondly, she uses the article, or, if plural, the adjective as a clue to the gender of the head noun, not the noun itself. The first of these might be defended on the grounds that practice should be directed where it is needed, in this case to the formal and orthographic alterations, and to insist that the problem be linked to a level of meaning might confuse the student and waste time. Some, but not all, behaviourist theorists might adopt this argument. The second indicates that she has realised that, in French, adjectives are more consistently marked by inflection for gender than nouns are. This is a useful piece of knowledge for a learner when faced with similar tasks. Of course, we do not know if these tactics were invented by the child alone or suggested by the teacher. However, it seems that what the student is practising is a set of well-founded and economical tactics for solving repetitive mechanical problems. From the psychological point of view we need to know more about such problem-solving strategies, and from the pedagogical point of view we need to decide whether the problems given to the students encourage the development of language proficiency or merely make further problems of the same type easier to solve. In the examples given by Hosenfeld the pupils' solutions appear to lead to further success in similar problems but not necessarily to language proficiency.

Problem-Solving and Concept Formation

Early research on problem-solving (see Woodworth and Schlosberg, 1955, ch. 26) was conducted by workers such as Maier and Duncker within the loose framework of Gestalt psychology. This school tended to emphasise the search for sense and symmetry in people's approaches to confusing or problematic situations rather than their use of environmental incentives. Maier's own experiments involved a simple mechanical puzzle in which two strings were suspended from the ceiling so widely apart that one person could not hold both of them at once; the task was to tie them together. There were several other objects in the room, and there were several possible solutions to the problem. One of these was to take a heavy object like a pair of pliers, tie it to one string and set it swinging like a pendulum, and then hold the other at full stretch and wait for the first string to swing into your hands. About 39 per cent of all the subjects thought of this without any help; 37 per cent were successful after some kind of guidance, consisting of the experimenter either 'accidentally' brushing past one of the strings and setting it swinging, or pointing out the pliers as the most useful adjunct; the rest failed. Despite the crudity of the experimental methodology, this simple demonstration convinced Maier of three quite important points. First, that there is obviously considerable individual variation in problem-solving ability; other Gestaltist writers, notably Wertheimer, speculated on how to encourage children in educational settings to gain experience of problem-solving and thus learn to think. Secondly, the problem appeared to be solved in a discontinuous fashion; there would be a number of false starts and blind alleys until there occurred a moment of insight, for example, into the pendulum principle or the utility of pliers as a weight rather than as pliers *per se*. The Gestaltists emphasised that this moment of insight or 'aha' experience involved a translation or transformation of the original view of the situation into a new one and they used the terms 'recentring' or 'cognitive restructuring' to describe this. Such terms still have an intuitive satisfaction but they do not constitute an explanation; later researchers have tried to find tasks which leave a continuous protocol of what the solver has done. Thirdly, the appearance of a new way of looking at the situation could not be attributed to reward or S–R associative bonds being established, since nothing of the sort was provided. Free association of otherwise distinct objects or functions of objects is a different matter.

More modern experiments with problem-solving have attempted to reveal the anatomy of the solving process, mainly by making the solver's covert decisions, backtrackings and intermediate solutions public, in the form of a detailed record of choices of certain courses of action and by actually controlling the sequence of information that is exposed to the solver.

Before looking at some examples of this work, it is as well to consider at what point in language learning this type of non-rewarded learning probably takes place. Dakin (1973) argued that every time a learner encounters an unfamiliar way of coding a meaning distinction in the new language, he has to apply puzzle-solving routines to make sense of it. Thus the fact that, in English, nouns but not names are marked with a preposed determiner (*the* or *a*) according to whether they are felt to be definite (*the man in blue danced a jig*), previously singled out (*I saw a man steal a coat. The thief ran off*), or unspecific (*a lion has escaped*), and are not so marked if they are felt to be generic (for example, *that's life*) presents a considerable problem to most non-native learners, since the rules for determiners in most other languages are rather different, if a recognisable determiner is present at all. Naturally this sort of problem is a far cry from joining two bits of string, but there are instructive similarities between the way people approach these tasks, the way they use and transform information, store it and retrieve it when appropriate and sometimes fail to do so.

A learner being exposed to the complexities of English article usage needs to have some way of collecting the various examples that he hears or reads and of inventing a set of principles or 'rules of thumb' which will simplify the issue for him and help him use the appropriate determiner when he himself speaks. It is irrelevant, for the moment, whether these principles are actually formulated into words by the learner, or given to him in words by the teacher, or indicated by coloured printing or diagrams. The question is, how does the process of attaining the understanding of the underlying regularities work? With a complex rule or system such as article use there are many ideas which a learner may entertain about parts of it which will be abandoned or modified later in the light of new information. This process is usually described as 'the creation of interim hypotheses' and the use of later information to decide what to do with them 'hypothesis testing'. Cognitive-code language teaching (see Chastain, 1971 and Lugton, 1971) has usually involved reliance on this sort of active mental participation by the learner. It is, perhaps, more important to realise that even in ostensibly behaviourist types of instruction students will be trying to make sense of the fragments of the language structure they are given although the conditions for successful hypothesis testing may not be present, and that therefore active processing may eventually be discouraged. The conditions for success are, or course, the opportunity to test hypotheses with evidence, that is, new information and the provision of feedback. Since many audio-lingual drills did not allow a creative response from the learner there was often no opportunity to try out a new bit of language which had been deduced from an idea about the structure being learnt; and frequently feedback was restricted to indications of success or reward rather than detailed information.

In a very thorough investigation of the attainment of concepts (albeit of a highly abstract kind to eliminate extraneous sources of guidance such as the subjects' everyday knowledge of the world and their language) Bruner, Goodnow and Austin (1958) demonstrated how different subjects coped with the three main limitations on puzzle-solving behaviour: limitations that computer puzzle-solvers do not suffer from. The three limitations, between which a delicate balance has to be struck, concern memory load, risk and the maximisation of information. A problem-solver must constantly bear in mind a considerable amount of information from earlier in the solution, which is continually being added to; at any moment a piece of information that earlier was thought insignificant may gain new importance. This load can easily grow too large to be constantly reviewed, even if it is transferred to paper; consequently, solvers invent strategies for keeping it to manageable proportions. A solver also has to undergo a certain amount of risk in the sense that making a particular choice or prediction may cost a great deal of effort and time if it proves to be a blind alley. A solver is also bound to try and get the maximum amount of information he can out of each opportunity. These three limitations are to some extent interdependent; to maximise information is to risk memory overload; to reduce what is to be held in memory might result in throwing away or ignoring key information. Bruner, Goodnow and Austin studied people's behaviour in an abstract version of the game 'I-Spy'. They found that their subjects differed markedly in the strategies they adopted to attain the geometrical concepts in their experimental design. The differences in strategy represented different solutions to the problem of overcoming the three limitations on problem-solving. Another important result was the subjects' reaction to disconfirmation or negative feedback when they were told that a particular card did not contain an instance of the concept. Logically one would expect a solver who was maximising information and concerned to reduce memory load consciously to solicit disconfirmation, as its value as information is considerably higher than that of confirmation. This is so because if a feature is thought to be important, and then is disconfirmed, all future instances of that feature can be ignored and all hypotheses using the feature eliminated; whereas if it is confirmed, more trials with that feature are still necessary to establish the concept.

Our reluctance to expose ourselves to negative feedback even when it is logically more useful, or even essential, was highlighted in an experiment by Wason (1964). He required subjects to think up a rule which the sequence of digits 2, 4, 6 obeys and to continue offering possible instances of this rule for feedback until they were certain they had found the actual rule in the experimenter's mind. An analogous language learning task would be to imagine that there were several possible explanations of why 'travelling' is spelt with a double 'l'; only one of them fits all the facts.

The simplicity of this experiment belies its importance; it reveals several characteristic types of behaviour. First, subjects tend to look only for verification, thus confirming the previous results of Bruner, Goodnow and Austin. Thus the majority of subjects, believing that the rule is 'any series of three ascending by two each time', will test this by proposing as instances, for example, 14, 16, 18, or 3, 5, 7, and will of course hear that these are correct. Few subjects attempt to test such a rule by inviting negative feedback with, say, 1, 2, 3 or 5, 8, 11. If these are disconfirmed the two-jump hypothesis can be held with confidence; if not, it must mean that an interval of two is irrelevant. In fact, two jumps are also acceptable. However, if a subject is asked to state why he advanced them as possible instances, he will be told that his rule is incorrect. Wason's rule is, in fact, simply 'any ascending set of three digits'. In other words, correct instances can be produced for the wrong reasons. Correct reasons (that is, rules rather than instances generated by the rules) can only be found if the risk of error is run. Secondly, the search for positive feedback can produce failure to sift irrelevant from relevant features. Thus discrimination learning must also involve potential negative feedback. Thirdly, Wason observed that many of the hypotheses that people put forward after a disconfirming response were in fact the same hypotheses in different words and led to more of the same sorts of suggested instances.

Dakin (1973) translated these insights into the inductive reasoning process into language teaching techniques. Although his book is ostensibly about language laboratory materials and their design the points he makes are also relevant to conventional classroom presentation. He argues that in order to understand and produce answers to problems students need to be set traps which will expose the nature of their hypotheses, of their developing understanding of the point at issue. The purpose of such traps is not to give the student discouragement or a sense of insecurity, which they need not do, but to create the conditions for negative feedback which unaided problem-solvers are somewhat reluctant to seek. If students are invited to make typical mistakes when forming their understanding of a language point the corrective feedback can come in time to prevent the formation of persistent misconceptions and resulting errors.

Dakin's own examples are given in an artificial language, Novish, but here is a possible adaptation of his method for teaching English. In teaching the difference between *since* and *for* with time expressions, one might begin by inviting inspection of two sets of rather similar sentences:

Set I   1 *John has lived in London for ten years.*

        2 *Mary has played the piano for fifteen years.*

        3 *Andrew has been learning to drive for six months.*

        4 *Tom has been going to school for one term.*

Set II   1 *William has lived in Edinburgh since 1968.*

2 *David has played the guitar since childhood.*

3 *Gordon has been learning to ride since Christmas.*

4 *James has been in prison since 1970.*

After comparing the two sets of sentences, students are invited to choose *since* or *for* in appropriate contexts. In other words, they have to decide what the basis for the difference between Sets I and II is, and apply it to a new sentence. There are, of course, a number of possible candidates; the sentence chosen for presentation should not contain obvious confounding but irrelevant differences, like having all Set I in the past tense but all Set II in the present perfect tense. One might proceed as follows:

Q1: Do we use *since* or *for* in the following?
  9 *Anna has been married —— seven years.*
  10 *Jeff has spent his holidays in Spain —— three years.*

Comment: These both have *for*. The Set I examples have time words and specific amounts; Set II time words are of a different sort. If you thought that *for* is used for lengths of time such as years, months, days, you were right.

Q2: What about this?
  11 *George has come to England —— a while to learn English.*

Comment: If you thought that *for* was only used when actual numbers of time units were given, you were wrong.

Q3: What about the following?
  12 *Anna has been married —— 1971.*
  13 *Jeff has gone to Madrid every year —— his twentieth birthday.*

Comment: These both have *since*. The difference between Sets I and II is the difference between *seven years, three years* and *1971, 1975*. Look back at the original eight sentences and think what this difference really is.

Q4: Do we use *since* or *for* here?
  14 *Victoria and Albert have loved each other —— the moment they met.*

Comment: since

Q5: Do we use *since* or *for* here?
  15 *Henry and Jane have kept the car —— a period of two years.*

Comment: *for.* 14 and 15 use more general time words.

Q6: So far, all the sentences have used the present perfect tense. What about these?
   16 *Last year, Michael was in Portsmouth —— two days.*
   17 *Next week, Concorde will be over Colchester —— half a second.*

Comment: They both take *for.* The time (past, present or future) within which the relevant period occurs is irrelevant.

Q7: Can you decide which preposition is needed here?
   18 *Peter has come here —— the summer ...*

Comment: Both are possible; the meanings are different. Write two completions, which make the two meanings clear.

Of course in a real situation more examples and very much more practice would be required; this is merely one example of how the student's reasoning may be guided so that misconceptions can be forestalled and problems solved with the support of the teacher. This also ignores the vexed question of whether the discussion about the new language point should be in the native or the foreign language; this would depend upon the particular teaching situation. In this type of presentation, potential mistakes are provoked and guidance given; the last step illustrated represents an attempt to get the student away from thinking in terms of a simple syntactic or morphological signal for the choice of preposition and into a consideration of semantic interpretations. Other linguistic considerations, such as the relationship of this small point to other time prepositions and the use of tenses, are ignored here.

There would have been many other ways of presenting this material so as to stimulate and guide the student's problem-solving activity. One alternative which is popular is to state the rule first and then show how it is exemplified. There are several reasons why this method may have unfortunate consequences. First, it is unlikely that the students can understand the rule statement until they have tested it against the various examples; but they may learn the rule statement verbatim without paying attention to the examples. Secondly, it imposes a rule formulation rather than encouraging the student to make one up in his own terms. In cases where the discrimination necessary is relatively simple, an imposed classification is usually less easy to remember and therefore less efficient than one invented for oneself (Mandler and Pearlstone, 1966). Where the rule to be assimilated is long and complex, in other words, where there are several contingencies and exceptions to the main principle, an imposed rule may have an advantage. However, this depends crucially on the manner and type of the guidance given. Another alternative to the illustrated steady unfolding of points, constructed according to some preconceptions about possible errors, would be the presentation of all the examples at once. While this would, logically, expose the student to the same information and allow him to work out the relevant generalisation, it would afford no guidance beyond the selection of relevant items and it would not allow the teacher to manage the problem-solving process.

Finally, it must be obvious that this type of presentation assumes that the learning of a language is aided if the task is broken down and focussed on specific points; and that part of the process involves the discovery and formulation of principles or rules. The first assumption will be looked at a little later in this chapter in relation to the old debate between 'part' and 'whole' methods of training. The second will be examined more closely in the chapter on second language acquisition. Dakin's position on this point can be seen in this quotation:

> The understanding of principles and the formulation of rules are the immediate object of problems. They are ... only an intermediate aid in language learning. Ultimate success depends not on the rules being followed to the letter, but on their becoming unnecessary: the learner can perform correctly without bothering to think why or how. (Dakin, 1973, p. 163)

The question that remains is whether in the specific case of language learning a stage of rule learning and formulation is necessary at all. This will be taken up again.

Types of Information

So far in this chapter, in contrast to Chapter 2, hardly any mention of reward has been made. Instead, 'information' has been used frequently. Psychologists have long distinguished between three different kinds of effects accruing from knowledge of results of actions. These are (Annett, 1969) (1) reinforcing, or drive-reducing effects, in which the receiving of some reward reduces the need which gave rise to the learning; (2) incentive, or drive-inducing effects, in which the provision of knowledge of results increases the probability of learning. 'An incentive is in some sense the promise which produces changes in behaviour before any reward is given' (Annett, 1969, p. 109); (3) informational effects, in which learning is promoted solely by the degree by which the learner's uncertainty about the difference between his performance and the required performance is reduced, and not by recourse to motivational effects like the first two.

In any normal educational setting all three types of effect are probably present when a teacher gives knowledge of results to a student. Giving an indication that the pronunciation of some word was better than it had been the previous week (1) rewards the student (at least if the student attributes the improvement to his own effort: see the later chapter on motivation) and possibly therefore slows down the rate of progress, (2) gives him an incentive that may prompt him to make similar efforts to improve other aspects of his performance (other aspects because it is unlikely that one piece of information would both increase and decrease the drive to improve the same performance) and (3) gives him an idea of the direction in which his performance was changing, in this case towards a standard desired by the teacher.

Knowledge of results and the various effects it has can be modelled theoretically in terms of a 'feedback loop' system. In such a system, there is a cycle of information-gathering, evaluation and action. Information is fed back for evaluation, action is taken, then information about the result of the action is again fed back; and so the cycle continues. Such devices (an oven thermostat is a simple kind) are called self-regulating servo-mechanisms. Considering human learning processes in the light of this analogy has been useful for several reasons. First, it enabled much more flexible and sophisticated forms of learning to be analysed, for which the simple models of response strength were inadequate. Secondly, it allowed consideration of all the effects of knowledge of results, namely reinforcement, incentive and uncertainty reduction. Thirdly, it provided a common theoretical umbrella under which studies of phenomena like learning, memory, attention, problem-solving and skill acquisition, which had largely been treated in isolation, could be considered in a common language. Lastly, information could be seen as a variable in its own right. This immediately eliminated the problem of incidental learning, referred to in Chapter 2, since although no reward was present, information certainly was. If information could be considered in its own right then it could also be considered in other circumstances than following an action: in other words, not simply as knowledge of results. For example, one can teach by modelling the desired performance. Modelling is in fact often used: most drills begin by presenting a model of what is intended should happen (model in the sense of guidance as to what is expected, not only samples of the language). This is a case where information is not presented as a consequence of action, but as a guide or prompt for action. In several laboratory experiments on maze learning (Von Wright, 1957) it has been shown that this technique is at least as effective as, or superior to, giving knowledge of results. With more complicated tasks there is a problem of transfer between the performance of what has been modelled and the use of that knowledge in other situations. Thus modelling a language structure is unlikely to lead to appropriate use of the structure in free conversation, whereas guided discovery of the underlying principle might, since it manages the kind and timing of information given to the student carefully and leaves the student a certain amount of control over the process. Good and Brophy (1978), however, suggest that problem-solving may itself be modelled by a teacher demonstrating and showing the students how to solve problems and find generalisations by asking crucial questions.

Language Learning as Skill Learning

It has often been remarked that learning a second language is different both from learning a first language and from learning other school subjects, because the students are learning a perceptuo-motor skill. In acquiring their first language, as well as learning the language code and how to use it to make utterances, children learn many other associated things, such as the management of social relationships and interaction, ways of categorising and viewing the world, and so on. To some extent the learner of a second language does not have to master all this, merely a new code. Other school subjects are sometimes called 'content' subjects, because what is taught is considered intellectually more substantial. Whether or not this is true, it has led to second language learning being thought of as adding a further social skill rather than as adding a new branch of knowledge to the student's repertoire. At the same time, little attention has been paid to the possible parallels between perceptuo-motor skill learning such as learning to drive, to fire a rifle, to draw, to typewrite, and so on, and the language skills. This might be because the word 'skill' is being used in two different senses, and information about the one is not relevant to the other, or because of less laudable reasons of accessibility or communication of research. In this section some of the parallels will be explored and illustrated. The literature on skill acquisition has been conspicuous for its development of the information-flow feedback model of learning.

Teachers have traditionally distinguished between receptive skills, namely, listening and reading, and productive skills, namely, speaking and writing, and cross-classified them into an oral-aural mode, speaking and listening, and a written mode, reading and writing. It is, however, doubtful that these four labels represent discrete skills. It is obvious that many of the components of the listening skill such as prediction, categorisation, segmentation, interpretation of ambiguity, and so on, are the same as occur in reading. Some of these questions will be taken up when we deal with production and comprehension of language. For the moment it is sufficient to note that a clear account of the psycholinguistic processes and their degree of commonality or overlap among the four skills would be pedagogically highly useful. It would enable us to decide to what extent it is reasonable to expect time spent on one type of activity to benefit another; and to what extent testing achievement in one area implies concomitant achievement in another area of language study: in other words, the problem of transfer.

Herriot (1971) and Levelt (1975) have proposed analyses of language learning in terms of skill acquisition. Both point out important features of skilled performance – feedback, anticipation, integration and hierarchical structure. Anticipation refers to the need to be ready for an action some time before it is required; a tennis player reads off the opponent's stroke where the ball is going to land and a language user reads off his interlocutor's intonation and eye movements, among other things, when his turn to speak is going to come. Hierarchical structure refers to the complex nature of most motor skills: they are organised in terms of plans which have as their components other plans. Thus changing gear in a car is part of a plan for increasing or decreasing road speed, and 'calls' or utilises a subplan for declutching at certain points which, however, is also 'called' during emergency braking. Language performance is also hierarchically structured in that certain elements may contain elements of the same kind, as when a relative clause is embedded in another one: *The dog which had eaten the fish which the cat wanted suffered.* In fact, language might be thought of as the most important and complicated kind of hierarchically structured behaviour that human beings engage in. The other significant fact about this type of behaviour is that elements low in the hierarchy can be performed automatically, that is, without conscious attention, freeing attention capacity for high-level decisions about communicative intent or message. Integration refers to the smooth operation of the various component parts of the hierarchy of decisions and is typical of skilled performance.

Many problems which are familiar in language teaching have been extensively researched in simpler skilled performances. One of the earliest observations, dating back to the last century (Bryan and Harter, 1899), was that with verbal material learning appears to slow down at various points, and if training is continued no appreciable improvement is made for a short time, after which it recurs. These periods were called 'plateaux'. They were observed in morse-code operators learning to receive code at high speeds. The explanation was that the learning plateaux coincided with changes in the way the operators received the morse signals – changes from hearing them as representing individual letters to hearing them as words and then as familiar phrases. When the new perceptual organisation was established, learning speed improved again. The phenomenon is familiar from language classrooms: some students – perhaps all – go through periods of time when they fail to learn anything more and may in fact backslide on items that previously were correct. This can be very dispiriting for the students concerned and can lead to dropping out. Keller (1958), working from a behaviourist standpoint, showed that a reanalysis of Bryan and Harter's data, and of several subsequent studies, cast doubt on whether the increase in speed of morse reception did follow this rather jerky pattern. Morse code, however, is only a recoding of individual letters, and the main variable is speed. It is quite possible that learning plateaux may exist in other, more complex kinds of learning, even if Keller was right about that particular learning situation. Indeed, more recent work on second language acquisition (for example, Hakuta, 1976) has established that decrement in performance (getting worse) can be evidence for learning. Hakuta's subject, Uguisu, a 5-year-old native speaker of Japanese, learned a complex structure quite early, the complement: *I know how to do it*; but her version of other variants of this complement were incorrect, and she subsequently changed the correct version, presumably by analogy with the invented question form, to: *I know how you do write this*. Later, the correct form in this type of sentence was re-established. Following similar reasoning in first language acquisition research, Hakuta interpreted this to mean that the first appearance of the correct form was as an unanalysed formula and the later, incorrect attempts were evidence of the setting up of a rule by which to produce utterances, which only later was perfected. Thus the interpretation of learning plateaux as evidence of internal reorganisation may after all be correct and, if this is so, it is even more reason to treat students who appear to be backsliding with special care.

Another long-standing problem in skill acquisition is whether it is better to break a task down into component parts or to teach it whole. The answer provided by Welford (1968, p. 291) is that learning the whole task at once, perhaps with slow presentation (time allowed for presentation is more useful than time allowed for recall), is preferable for highly co-ordinated activities (his example is flying an aircraft), whereas splitting the task up into components is preferable for tasks that are more like actions in a series or ordered sequence. Speaking a language would presumably fall into the first category; but just as one would not imagine that it was good practice to teach take-off, level flight and landing in the same lesson, so some breakdown of the total task is unavoidable. The question is, to what extent can language points be isolated without destroying the co-ordination of the system and the perception of what Corder (1974) called the 'systematic interconnectedness' of language? The problem of part versus whole learning is essentially the problem of integration of subcomponents. If the complexity of the task is relatively high, the evidence from perceptuo-motor skill learning implies that breaking it down will hinder development of the smooth integrated functioning of the whole. If it is low, or if the task is easily separated into a series of relatively independent subtasks, integration is aided by the division of training. This insight – in some ways a surprising one – offers a perspective on syllabus design which is not always attended to. For some years there has been discussion in a number of areas of applied linguistics of this part versus whole problem. It appears in the field of language testing in the much discussed distinction between tests of discrete point items and tests of integrative skills. In the former, test batteries are thought to consist of numbers of independent molecular items, usually of structure, phonology or vocabulary. In the latter, tests are constructed according to the assumption that language skills are essentially indivisible and that language performance involves using all the relevant knowledge and skills in interpreting a text or in actual conversation. Broadly, the two modes of testing reflect different beliefs about language performance: the former, that performance is the sum of all the individual independent items of knowledge and detailed skills, the latter, that performance is the integration of interdependent knowledge and skill. The argument in the field of testing can be independent of similar distinctions in the field of learning but, in fact, the part versus whole distinction has received considerable attention in the literature on teaching methods and course design. Workers both in foreign language teaching and in the teaching of reading have contrasted synthetic with analytic methods. Synthetic methods take a prior division of the material into small, relatively independent units (in foreign language teaching, usually syntactic patterns; in the teaching of reading, individual sounds or letters) and teach them in a graded sequence. Analytic methods take larger and more heterogeneous teaching units that are more like large chunks of language (for example, whole texts). Several different kinds of analytic, or holist, approach have been suggested and following Wilkins (1976) one can list as the basic material round which the teaching units are organised: (a) rich chunks of language; (b) situations, where the teaching and learning unit is designed to teach some representative sample of the language needed for a particular situation (such as 'at the bank', 'buying a house', 'in the dock'); (c) notions, where the unifying principle of each teaching and learning unit is a particular semantic intention, and the language taught may be many ways of expressing the same semantic intention and the distinctions between the appropriateness of each expression in different contexts (examples of notions would be time, deixis, mood or persuading, requesting, greeting). The fact that the results in skill acquisition favour whole over part learning where the total body of knowledge is highly complex is very relevant here, since such a large part of what have become known as notional-functional syllabuses have to do with social, that is, interpersonal, skills in the new language. One further, and rather different, interpretation of holist learning can be found in the suggestion that foreign languages should be taught intensively over periods of days rather than hours, often using the foreign language as the medium of instruction for other curriculum subjects. Of course, this kind of suggestion involves more than the part versus whole learning distinction, such as the motivational effects of using the foreign language for communication where the language is not the object of study. Several experiments in schools, where for a number of days all subjects are taught in a foreign language (see Lambert and Tucker, 1972) have shown that where the organisational difficulties can be overcome, the benefits in foreign language achievement are great, and do not subtract from the achievement in the other subjects.

A third familiar problem in both skill acquisition and language learning is that of sequencing tasks that differ in difficulty. The usual assumption in language teaching syllabuses has been that there should be a steady gradation from easy to difficult, so that the most difficult items and skills are reserved for the time when the students have most experience in the language. In this way, with increased difficulty being matched by increased experience, the level of difficulty as perceived by the student should remain approximately constant. Much effort has gone into finding criteria for the grading of language structures, skills and situations and, more recently, functions, in order to put this principle into practice. It is the principle behind the frequent use of the language of demonstration (*This is a* ——, *That is a* ——) in the first lessons, and the postponement of subordination (by relative pronoun and conjunctions of time, manner, purpose, concession, and so on) until after the tense system, the noun phrase, modal verbs and some adverbs have been taught. No doubt it is a good pedagogic principle for syllabuses in the long term. In the short term, however, it is not supported by evidence from studies of skill acquisition. In laboratory experiments it has been found (Welford, 1968, p. 311) that if subjects have to learn two tasks differing in difficulty, it is usually more efficient to learn the more difficult one first, as the greater care and attention demanded will benefit the learning of the easy task more than having an easy run will help the difficult task. Welford summarises the results of several types of experiment thus: 'If two or more tasks have to be learnt, it is most beneficial to begin with the one which elicits the greatest care and effort towards the attainment of a high standard of performance.' He adds the rider that this principle is true for those cases where sufficient practice at the more difficult task is given for 'reasonable mastery'. If this is not done the learner is left with insufficient comprehension of the task and the beneficial effect on the second task is lost. Of course, this result cannot be invoked to support the reversal of a three-year school syllabus in order to start with tasks usually thought of as the culmination; but there is no reason why in restricted areas of the syllabus this somewhat surprising principle cannot be used to upset the traditional tight upward grading and to release from teacher control, with the benefit of faster learning and student success. For example, Tongue *et al.* (1977) suggest that teaching written composition should progress from 'controlled' through 'guided' to 'free' expression (that is, with a continually and smoothly decreasing degree of teacher guidance) and they exemplify this principle in a remarkably full and elaborated set of sample materials for use in South East Asia. However, it could be argued that writing skills might be acquired more efficiently if such a course were interrupted at different points for the students to attempt assignments of a more difficult level than their current stage of progress; these would act as a stimulus and a challenge to raise performance on subsequent easier tasks when the normal sequence was resumed. This would naturally be subject to the condition that the language of the more difficult tasks was itself within the capacity of the students.

Summary

This chapter has examined something of what is known about human problem-solving and hypothesis testing and related it to students' active search for regularities in the language material they are exposed to. The notion of guided discovery was looked at and in particular the role of guidance in provoking possible incorrect hypotheses and forestalling errors. The information-processing model of psychological functioning was introduced in general terms and parallels were drawn between language learning and the acquisition of perceptuo-motor skills.

Chapter 4

Comprehension and Production of Language

This chapter examines some of the results of work on the psychological processes engaged when a listener or reader attempts to understand a stretch of language and when a speaker or writer produces some language with a communicative intention. It would be tempting to argue that there is but one set of processes, which can be operated in two directions: in one way as a set of instructions for planning and executing utterances, leading from a level of ordered thoughts to a level of phonetic instructions, or pronunciations; and also the other way round, as a set of interpretive devices leading from a level of acoustic sensation to a level of ordered thoughts. Early psycholinguistic theories tended to make this assumption. However, later work, while not denying certain fundamental parallels, has emphasised the differences between the two situations, and it is preferable to speak of two sets of processes.

In terms of the framework established in the introductory chapter information about these processes contributes to the analysis of competent performance. From this analysis can be derived justifications for schemes of work designed to encourage pupils to develop the communicative skills of language and exercises for developing particular strategies of interpretation.

Psycholinguistic Assumptions

Of course, this is not a new suggestion; assumptions about psychological processes have always been present in decisions about course materials and teaching strategies, often without the teacher being aware of them. For example, one might contrast two possible methods of teaching the form of the passive in English, both of which have been used in EFL texts. Method A introduces the passive by way of copula and adjective constructions:

    A1   *John is cheerful*

perhaps also using adjectives ending in *-ed* derived from intransitive verbs:

A2 *John is relaxed.*

and in a later lesson substitute transitive verbs:

A3 *John is beaten.*

Finally, after plenty of practice at that, an agentive *by* phrase is added:

A4 *John is beaten by Mary.*

Method B takes as its starting point a simple active declarative sentence with a transitive verb:

B1 *Cats eat fish.*

Questions are asked which focus on particular parts of the sentence, first of all the object or goal of the verb:

B2 Q: *What do cats eat?*
    A: *Fish.*

After a lesson putting the object to the front, the next step is number concord in the auxiliary:

B3 Q: *What are tasty for cats?*
    A: *Fish are (tasty).*

The form of the participle has to be introduced:

B4 Q: *What happens to the fish?*
    A: *Fish are eaten.*

Finally the original actor reappears in the *by* phrase:

B5 Q: *What are eaten by cats?*
    A: *Fish are eaten by cats.*

In exploitation, all four formal changes are practised in one so-called transformation drill.

If either or both of these methods of introducing the passive voice work as teaching devices it must be because they expose the student to a number of palatable half-truths about English sentence structure. Method A pretends that there is a structural and functional equivalence between copula + adjective and auxiliary + participle constructions (transitive and intransitive), the passive being completed by the addition of a *by* ——

phrase. Method B pretends that passives are formed from actives by the stated formal manipulations. These may be very useful assumptions which simplify the task for the student. Presumably the exercises forming the class activities for each method are designed to practise the principle upon which each is based. If that is so, then the users of each method assume that they reflect, in outline, the process by which proficient speakers of the language form, and in reverse, comprehend passives. Such an assumption seems to be the only justification for constructing the syllabus in that way. Those assumptions can, however, be put to experimental test; in this particular case, neither of them is wholly justified. (However, it is interesting that native children seem to acquire control over passive forms in a similar sequence to that of Method A: see Chapter 7, p. 99.) Note that the failure of experimentation to justify the assumptions of a pedagogic technique does not of itself discredit the technique as pedagogy; however, the limitations of the technique can be more clearly seen. In this case, one might continue using one or other of these techniques as a simplification for beginners, building into a later part of the course an opportunity for the students to reformulate their plans for passives. This is one of the advantages of a cyclic syllabus.

The Search for Psychological Reality

Some of the earliest psycholinguistic experiments concentrated on the relationship between psychological processes in expressing and extracting meaning in language and formal grammatical descriptions of language structure. The linguists themselves were careful to point out that in principle linguistic theories did not claim to be psychological theories. However, it was recognised that linguistic theories, by extending the breadth and depth of the available descriptions of language structure, might hold serious implications for psychological studies of language processes. There is no space here for a detailed consideration of the various schools of linguistic theory since 1950, and the reader is referred to the excellent introductions by Dinneen (1967), or Lyons (1968), or Wilkins (1972).

The theory that most attracted psychologists was that being developed by Chomsky (1957), partly because of the feeling that this provided a way of measuring language processes beyond the simple counting of words or other units and partly because of Chomsky's own challenging rebuttal of behaviourist conceptions of language in his review (1959) of Skinner's *Verbal Behaviour*. Some of those arguments we have already examined in Chapter 2. Broadly speaking, Chomsky's theory of syntax contained two sets of rules. One set described common features of all sentences (such as the relation of subject and predicate, of verb and object, of adjective and noun) and the other described distinguishing features of different types of sentences (such as passive forms, negative forms, relative clauses, question forms). The two sets were interrelated so that the grammar could describe both what was shared between (a) and (b) and (c) and (d) below, and also what was different:

(a) *Bill hit the ball*
(b) *The ball was hit by Bill*
(c) *Was the ball hit by Bill?*
(d) *Wasn't the ball hit by Bill?*

Furthermore, sentence (d) was described as being related to sentence (a) via the two intervening sentences, in that order. This was called the 'derivational history' of the sentence.

Miller (1962) suggested that this grammatical theory might provide a model of part of the psychological process of comprehension or production if one could show that the linguists' descriptive rules for interrelating these sentences (called transformational rules) were equivalent to psychological work, in other words, that transformations were actual mental operations. Specifically he proposed that in order to understand (d) *Wasn't the ball hit by Bill?* we uncover the basic sentence (a) *Bill hit the ball* by working backwards through the derivational history (the rules by which the sentence was originally formed), making a mental note of what they were for future reference:

Hear:	*Wasn't the ball hit by Bill?*	
Convert to:	*The ball wasn't hit by Bill*	+ question
Convert to:	*The ball was hit by Bill*	+ question + negative
Convert to:	*Bill hit the ball*	+ question + negative + passive

Work out the meaning of the basic sentence.

Initial experimental results with this simple theory (Miller and McKean, 1964, Savin and Perchonock, 1965) were encouraging, both with time and memory measures. This was taken to mean that despite the linguists' disclaimers grammatical descriptions at least of the Chomskyan type were also descriptions of psychological processes and could be empirically tested as such.

However, this simple version of the idea of psychological reality was soon shown to be seriously wrong. First, it predicted that certain sentences should have been more difficult to understand than people usually judge them to be, on the grounds that their derivational history was longer (that is, contained more transformations of structure). For example,

(1)   *It is obvious that Hazel was amazed that David wanted to go*

should have been more difficult to comprehend than

(2)   *That that David wanted to go amazed Hazel is obvious*

and this is contrary to most people's judgement. The reason is that the theory does not take account of the fact that structural choices, like putting a clause into the passive, or taking a clause out of another clause and putting it outside with an *it* (called 'extraposing') are not arbitrary but are performed for particular reasons. In this case, putting the three simple active declarative kernel sentences

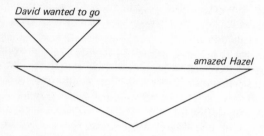

together in a complex active declarative sentence produces the peculiarly difficult sentence (2). Quite why this sort of clause-within-a-clause-within-a-clause structure is difficult to grasp is poorly understood; it appears to violate some basic limitation of our memory for speech. In the grammatical theory which Miller based his early experiments on (N. Chomsky, 1957) further transformations were necessary to form (1) out of the basic structure of (2) by passivising *amazed Hazel* and extraposing *it is obvious*, thus avoiding the peculiar difficulty of (2). Of course, the result is paradoxical; the linguistic theory adds transformations whose result appears to be a sentence which is easier to comprehend, but the psychological theory based on it holds that this should result in sentences that are more difficult to comprehend.

Secondly, the theory ignored the situation of the utterance. People choose sentence mood (negative, affirmative, and so on) and voice (active, passive) for particular pragmatic purposes; a negative sentence is usually used when there is a reason to negate some fact or assumption and passives are used in order to make the object or goal the topic of the sentence:

The ball was hit by John

or when the agent is either not known:

Money has been stolen from the bank

or is to be suppressed:

The experiment was performed.

Several experiments have shown that in situations where these conditions are satisfied, these sentence types are no more difficult to understand or produce than the simple active declarative sentence in its appropriate circumstances (Wason, 1965).

Many other criticisms of the derivational theory of complexity as a psychological theory have been advanced, and can be read in Fodor and Garrett (1966), and other sources. There are implications for language teaching even in this somewhat negative assessment of the early psycholinguistic work. It seems that the assumption that structural manipulation drills bear any close relationship to actual language behaviour is untenable. The alternative justification for them, that they are an easily understood way of getting learners to use certain structures, in other words, that they are pedagogically convenient, loses much of its force if the first assumption is no longer believed since there can be no guarantee of transfer of training to other situations. The related question of the relationship between structural complexity and learning difficulty has also been thrown open to question. Whereas it used to be assumed that the greater the degree of linguistic complexity in a sentence the more difficult it would be to produce or understand and therefore to learn, the failure of the derivational theory to explain production or understanding has shown that this assumption is not justified. Linguistic complexity is often the cost incurred in making messages easier to understand, by arranging elements of the message in a particular sequence. Naturally it is still the case that learning to arrange elements of information in this way and therefore engaging more complex syntactic constructions such as passives and subordinating clauses may be difficult. The early psycholinguistic experimentation has at least shown why. This whole issue is an aspect of the organisation of language for communicative function, which will be taken up again in Chapter 6.

Comprehension as Construction

Such considerations, as well as the major and rapid development within linguistic theory in the 1960s and 70s, led to the abandonment of the idea that linguistic rules, at least in the forms then envisaged, represented psychological processes. In its place there was proposed (Bever, 1970) a much looser relationship between the two: a set of interpretive strategies, or heuristic devices, operating on the text as heard (or read) and producing, or constructing, a representation of the meaning of the text by reference to (a) the cues in the text itself (b) the rules of the grammar of the language and (c) relevant knowledge from memory. Clark and Clark (1977, p. 49) give a simple outline of the construction process:

(1)   [Listeners] take in the raw speech and retain a phonological representation of it in 'working memory'.

(2)   They immediately attempt to organise the phonological representation

into constituents, identifying their content and function.

(3)   As they identify each constituent, they use it to construct underlying propositions, building continually on to a hierarchical representation of propositions.

(4)   Once they have identified the propositions for a constituent, they retain them in working memory and at some point purge memory of the phonological representation. In doing this, they forget the exact wording and retain the meaning.

These four steps in sentence perception present a rather different, and more complicated, picture than that outlined in the previous section. The first point to notice is that this approach views comprehension as a process in which the listener does a great deal of work, building meanings from sounds. For foreign language learner who is not proficient at listening comprehension needs exercises aimed at developing his skills in performing this work.

This simple suggestion of the Clarks serves to illustrate the contrast between the approach discussed in the last section, which emphasised the derivational history of the sentences, and the constructivist approach. However, it immediately raises two major questions in the light of which we must examine the evidence. One may question the order in which the steps are applied, if indeed the intervening steps are applied in any consistent order, and one may question the validity of the steps themselves. In this section and the following one on reading comprehension we shall look at some of the evidence for syntactic and semantic processing strategies and for processing from individual sound or letter to sense (bottom to top) or vice versa (top to bottom).

The first step will be looked at in greater detail in the next chapter, when different types of memory are discussed, but one should note that many problems of the language learner result from making up faulty or incomplete phonological representations. The student does not succeed in identifying the speech sounds correctly and there are several reasons for this. One is speed; another is a lack of built-in expectations about what words are likely to sound like in the foreign language. In English this problem is accentuated by the process of vowel reduction, whereby several syllables may contain the same vowel sound schwa / ə / dependent upon the position of the stressed syllable. Exercises in recognition of stress placement may well aid this identification process.

Evidence for the second step comes from Garrett, Bever and Fodor's click dislocation experiments, among other sources. In these experiments the old idea that perceptual units resist interruption (which goes back to Gestaltist psychology) and that therefore physically simultaneous stimuli are in fact perceived in series was applied to sentence constituents. Clicks superimposed on to a tape of a spoken sentence should be perceived at constituent boundaries whether they really occur there or in the middle of the constituent. For example, in Garrett, Bever and Fodor's (1966) experiment, a click superimposed on the tape at (*) should be perceived in different places according to the structure:

(1) *(As a result of their invention's influence) (the * company was given an award,*

(2) *(The chairman whose methods still influence the * company) (was given an award).*

In fact, the clicks were reported as occurring between *influence* and *the* in (1), and *company* and *was* in (2). In this particular experiment the underlined words were actually the same piece of tape, with different beginnings spliced on the front, so any difference must have been due to the subjects' imposition of constituent structure. A non-native speaker, of course, cannot rely on this intuitive working-out of constituent structure, and he makes many wrong decisions. The native speaker has a number of strategies available to him for this purpose. These may be conveniently, if informally, divided between syntactic strategies and semantic strategies. Syntactic strategies may be thought of as searching for particular syntactic clues such as conjunctions, relative pronouns, determiners (sometimes grouped together as 'function words' because they signal syntactic relations), and using them to set up expectations of what form-classes may follow, in order to parse, or recognise the syntax, of the major constituents and their relationships. There is some evidence for the existence of such strategies, both at the level of noun and verb phrases and at clause level. For example, Kimball (1973) showed that listeners identify function words and look for other words which are appropriate: find a 'the' and then look for a noun or a noun preceded by an adjective. Fodor, Garrett and Bever (1974) discuss the possibility that listeners assume that the first verb in a sentence is part of the main clause unless there is evidence to the contrary in the form of a conjunction or a relative pronoun.

Clearly, for the native speaker, these syntactic strategies are dependent upon knowledge of the grammar. Grammatical expectations lead to predictions about meaning relationships. One type of exercise which is designed to train the language learner to use to the maximum his knowledge of function words replaces the content words with pronounceable nonsense. For example, listen to the following passage:

Zigs

There are many kinds of zigs. Although the common domestic zig is best known for binting itself, prinning, and glucking, many elements of its behaviour are reminiscent of its larger and fiercer foger, which hunt other blicks for sog and frequently store the sog for later use by the family.

What can you say about *zigs* and *fogers*?

What does the speaker think of the *zigs', binting, prinning* and *glucking*?
(Key: *zig* = cat,   *binting* = washing,   *prinning* = sleeping,   *glucking* = purring, *foger* = cousin, *blick* = animal, *sog* = food)
(by analogy with 'Morts' by Sturtridge, McAlpin and Harper, 1974)

However, comprehension strategies relying on function words, affixes and inflections labour under the difficulty that in ordinary speech it is exactly those parts of the utterance that are most difficult to hear, because they are usually unstressed, spoken quickly and suffer vowel reduction. Also, they are usually the most predictable parts of the sentence.

The effects of stress placement and intonation on these elements can be offset for the non-native speaker by giving exercises in recognition of stress placement (for example, transcripts with stresses marked, or with gaps requiring completion with stressed words) and in the recognition of function words in relation to the intonation contour of the sentence.

The second difficulty leads to the second general class of strategies. There is evidence that when people try and interpret sentences they hear they sometimes look for content words and work out their possible meanings and then look for function words which signal appropriate syntactic relations between them. This would imply that syntactic analysis was a later stage than word meaning recognition and would account for the predictability of function words (because word meanings set up expectations for syntax). In one sense, this class of strategies is a reversal of steps (2) and (3) of the simple outline on pp. 45–6. The suggestion is that the first operation performed on the phonological representation is the recognition of content words, from which syntactic constituents may be built and then checked. This procedure would conform better to listeners' working beliefs that speakers are trying to make sense and that they are trying to express themselves in a comprehensible fashion. Clark and Clark suggest, among other strategies, the following: 'Using content words alone, build propositions that make sense and parse the sentence accordingly' (Clark and Clark, 1977 p. 73, Strategy 8). This strategy may be the factor that makes (a) easier than (b) in the following:

(a)   *The man the cat the dog barked at scratched spoke French.*
(b)   *The man the cat the dog saw heard ran away.*

Both of these, of course, are very peculiar because of the clause-within-a-clause-within-a-clause aspect discussed earlier. (a) sounds less peculiar than (b) because verbs can be matched up with agents uniquely, on the assumption that the speaker really was trying to make sense, whereas in (b) all the agents could perform the actions denoted by all the verbs.

Foreign language learners often fail to make sense of sentences in the new language in this way, although they use semantic strategies in their native language. This is often because they are not able to think of possible sense relations between words they know the meaning of in time to find syntactic features which would express those sense relations before the sentence fades from memory. Classroom time can be devoted directly to this process if the material to be interpreted is presented several times, for example, by playing the tape again. On first hearing, students are directed to note down or tick off on a list the content words they can understand, then to work out what possible interrelationships they have. On second hearing, their partial interpretation is checked against the tape for completeness.

In the four steps in comprehension quoted on pp. 45–6, step (3) consisted of building propositions from the constituents established in step (2) and finally in step (4) these were committed to a working memory and the verbatim record forgotten. Evidence for step (4) comes from Sachs (1967), who read people short passages followed by a test sentence, asking them if they recognised it from the passage. With almost any delay, but most dramatically after forty syllables, most people confuse with the original sentence a test sentence which is different in syntactic form but not in meaning, and do not confuse sentences which are different in meaning.

This phenomenon occurs most strongly when the original and the test sentences are separated by about forty syllables of other material. Bever (in Fodor, Garrett and Bever, 1974) has argued that people lose the verbatim record after each major clause boundary (unless they know they are going to be tested on it). How propositions function within the organisation of memory will be discussed in the next chapter; here it is important to show how information from earlier parts of the message interacts with new information in the construction of interpretations, that is, extracting from the language code the meat of the propositional content. In real life, as opposed to laboratory experiments, people are rarely called upon to comprehend single sentences uttered in a vacuum. They use information derived from what they have heard earlier to interpret what they are hearing now. They use various signals, sometimes called 'discourse markers', which speakers make to give what they are saying coherence and organisation, in order to build larger propositions which encompass the information from several sentences. Exactly what words signal these longer propositions depends on the type of discourse, but in an academic lecture they might be 'first', 'second', 'third', 'for example' or 'in conclusion' and in a story they might be various conventional phrases such as 'Once upon a time', 'dear reader', and so on. Several authorities have recently argued (for example, Kintsch, 1975) that the listeners are here constructing major propositions into which to set the individual points represented by sentences or clauses. We will see some examples of this macro-organisation of meaning in the next chapter.

An experiment by Bransford and Johnson (1972) demonstrates the extreme difficulty of listening to connected discourse when the listener has no clue at the beginning as to what sorts of information are going to be of value to him in constructing an interpretation. The following passage was read at normal conversational speed to two groups. One of the groups was told it was about washing clothes; the other was given no such title. Nothing else differed. The group given the title judged the passage to be fairly easy to comprehend and in fact remembered quite a lot of it; the group without a title judged it moderately difficult and remembered far less of it.

The procedure is actually quite simple. First, you arrange things into different groups. Of course, one pile may be sufficient depending on how much there is to do. If you have to go somewhere else due to lack of facilities that is the next step, otherwise you are pretty well set. It is important not to overdo things. That is, it is better to do too few things at once than too many. In the short run this may not seem important but complications can easily arise. A mistake can be expensive as well. At first the whole procedure will seem complicated. Soon, however, it will become just another facet of life. It is difficult to foresee any end to the necessity for this task in the immediate future, but then one can never tell. After the procedure is completed one arranges the materials into different groups again. Then they can be put in their appropriate places. Eventually they will be used once more and the whole cycle will have to be repeated. However, that is part of life.

I have conducted this experiment several times as a classroom demonstration and the result has always confirmed the original finding. This illustrates that part of the difficulty of listening comprehension lies in the opportunities available to the listener for setting up categories with which to organise a large amount of the more detailed information which is to follow. When these are not present the process of constructing propositions from constituents and macro-propositions from propositions is quite severely disturbed because, first, there are too many inchoate clues to the most coherent interpretation and, secondly, the listener has to focus his attention on finding candidates for the overall organisational categories, that is, he is too busy looking for the theme to process the details.

This effect recalls Ausubel's suggestion that, in reading, learners need 'advance organisers' by which to begin interpreting the text. In teaching listening comprehension these advance organisers come in the shape of word lists (in Widdowson's (1978) precise terms, 'priming glossaries'), short orienting reading passages, or short discussions about the topic. However, while exercises on individual stages in the listening process are important, more valuable is a scheme of work for integrating the various subskills into a coherent construction. In this connection see the article by J. McDonough (1978), which describes the construction of a graded set of exercises based on authentic lecture material.

Reading as a Constructive Process

It is perhaps less strange to talk of reading as a construction process than it is of listening. The idea that reading is a process of reasoning out what the author's intended message is, his attitude to it and the point that lies behind the message, from the cues presented in the actual orthography, is not a new one. However, the process is not necessarily exactly the same as in listening. Because the signs on the page have a permanence of their own it is not necessary to adopt strategies for rapid clause-by-clause analysis of a transient verbatim memory; the signs on the page can be visited and re-visited many times, both in advance of and immediately before the portion of text being read at any one moment. Studies of people's eye-movements while reading aloud have shown that, indeed, this is precisely what is happening, with a tendency for the eyes to be looking ahead more than behind. Thus the presence of a paper memory makes a difference to the kind of processing that is necessary. This is, of course, independent of the argument as to whether we translate the written symbols into sounds before performing syntactic and semantic analysis. The evidence on this point appears to be inconclusive (Levy, 1977). We may do so; it may be part of the reading process; but, equally, it may not be necessary.

A method of investigating the reading process which has had considerable success is categorising errors people make in reading aloud. Goodman (1973) has labelled this type of research 'miscue analysis'. The word 'miscue' refers to the use of cues in the text for making decisions about the text at various levels of abstraction and to the frequently observed failure to make the right decisions. The model of reading which Goodman uses he has called the 'psycholinguistic guessing game' (1967). In the spirit, but not in the details, of the previous discussion of listening, this is to be distinguished from word-by-word left-to-right processing, which is characteristic of the beginner and unsuccessful reader, but not of the mature reader. Rather, Goodman claims that his miscue analysis research shows that experienced readers (including children) sample the text continuously for cues on which to base interpretations, 'guided by constraints such as prior choices, language knowledge, cognitive style, and strategies they have learned'. The reader uses his knowledge of the redundancy, the predictability, of the language code to make informed guesses at the shape, constituent structure, syntax and meaning of the next piece of the text and then checks this guess with the actual text. Often the check is not thorough; if there is sufficient match between guess and symbols for an interpretation that makes sense to pass, attention will be moved to the next section. In an investigation of English reading by an Arabic-speaking child, Rigg (1976) points out: 'Three basic strategies – prediction, confirmation, and correction – help Leila to process the printed word quickly and meaningfully.' Here is an example of Rigg's subject reading a difficult sentence with all the miscues she committed:

3 *That was* (correct)
2 *th-*
1 *the n-* [non-word] *result*
   That was exactly the result which Fareedah had
2 *deserred* (non-word)
1 *de-*
   desired and she went to lie in the shade of a fig tree. In fact the lazy girl had
1 *cungly* (non-word)
   cunningly avoided all work for many years.

The miscues here all show use, albeit unsuccessful use, of cues at various levels, graphological (for example, the *-ngly* ending) and grammatical (for example, the past marker on the non-word *deserred*). An example of a semantic miscue from Rigg's subject is *You are not thinking of breaking our arrangement* instead of ... *our bargain.*

It is often felt that second language learners do not usually produce semantic miscues, being preoccupied with lower-level information – letter shapes, spelling, punctuation, syntax. If this is the case, it could be because they are often not encouraged to sample large enough portions of the text to allow semantic information, that is, ideas about the general meaning of the text, to be used in clarifying the muddles at those lower levels. Students who are constrained to use only local redundancy, that is, who are instructed to comprehend fully each phrase before going on to the next, necessarily have this more global source of information cut off from them. Successful readers use the semantic information to sort out the unfamiliar letter sequences or grammar which might be the source of error.

The parallel that exists here between semantic strategies in reading and semantic strategies in listening, discussed on pp. 106–7, underlines the great degree of commonality between the two processes. Some researchers have even argued that there is only one process of comprehension after the translation from a sound or a letter code into a constituent representation. However, one must not forget the transience of a sound message as compared to the permanent availability of a written message for checking and backtracking.

There have been several attempts to specify just what different levels of analysis, or stages in the construction process, there are in reading. Kintsch (1975), for example, gives the following list.

Visual code   (letter shapes)

Word identification (word shapes)

Syntax   (linguistic structure)

Semantics   (sense relations)

Pragmatics   (topic of discourse)

Function   (language use)

The last two may be unfamiliar. Pragmatic analysis refers to the building of larger units of meaning out of the sense relations expressed by individual sentences. Thus as we read stories, for example, we do not simply amass a long string of equally important pieces of information, but organise them into openings, episodes, flashbacks, resolutions, denouements, and so on. Similarly in other genres, such as newspaper reports, scientific report writing, letters, there are relatively well-known conventions concerning these larger units. On the printed page, they are sometimes indented as paragraphs. Functional analysis refers to the recognition by the reader of the effect that the author of the text is creating, and any decisions about the action the reader wishes to take: stop reading, reply, and so on.

Assuming the six levels of decision above are sufficient to capture the important stages of building interpretations of written material, two further points about the process are crucial. The first is that each stage calls on knowledge already stored in long-term memory: for example, word glosses, syntax, schemata for various types of organisation, schemata for the topic under discussion and previously held beliefs about the writer's intentions. The second is that processing may occur either way; technically, top-to-bottom and bottom-to-top. That is, a decision about the appropriate interpretation of a particular clause might as well be the result of syntactic and semantic analysis as derived from a recognition of what point in story structure had been reached and what the author was trying to say.

Reading, then, is a highly complex process, and the language teacher has a large array of possible exercise types designed to encourage the development of strategies at each level and their integration.

Before a text is read expectancies can be encouraged by adjunct questions which focus the reader's attention on finding the answers and by various word-finding techniques that prime the reader to be ready for particular words. If, however, such priming techniques effectively present all the new words in a passage the student is debarred from operating otherwise normal strategies for building meanings from context and thus from developing his own vocabulary-building strategies.

Perhaps the most popular kind of reading exercise consists of a passage, usually selected for its interest and degree of difficulty, followed by a number of questions. The questions may be of several types but the main purpose is to find out if comprehension has occurred. In fact, of course, it is not quite fair to regard this only as a testing exercise; the questions also act as guides for the students in building interpretations at the end of the passage. Frase (1972) and Rothkopf (1970) have both investigated the use of these test-like events in stimulating comprehension. One of their measures was the proportion of material related to the question and incidental material retained over a short delay of time. With adjunct questions, related material is recalled best; with post-text questions, the proportions are nearly equal. It is not clear from their results whether this difference is due to further processing while reading the text, before the post-text questions are known, or to the aid that the questions themselves provide. It is probably both.

However, such reading exercises have been criticised for not explicity encouraging positive learning strategies. Techniques for doing this may be divided into those that break up texts and those that construct texts. Examples in the first category would be (a) interspersed questions, where questions are inserted into the text asking for a decision referring back a few lines, or for a prediction of the next most likely events, which should be followed by interruptions of the text to require students to formulate their own relevant questions; (b) cloze procedure, where the use of local redundancy is required to fill in a gap with a word that is appropriate to the syntax, sense, and style of the passage. (There is an element of construction in cloze procedure which is worth noting: the greater the number of gaps filled, the more complete the text and the easier the remaining gaps are to fill); and (c) scrambled texts, where a paragraph of which the clauses are presented in random order has to be reconstituted by working out the correct or the original order of the clauses from cues of chronology, logical relations, anaphoric reference, word knowledge and textual cohesion markers, such as conjunctions of time, purpose, concession, phrases indicating comparison and contrast (*on the other hand* ...), and as many other cues as the readers find to help them. The pedagogic claim implicit in these sorts of exercise is that each in its own way encourages students to develop strategies of building interpretations based on a search for all the relevant cues in a text, which can generalise to all texts.

The second category of exercises, involving construction of a text, shares the assumption that the best way to become sensitive to all the cues necessary to build a coherent and valid interpretation is to participate in building the text which is to be interpreted. Several such techniques have been suggested short of the claim that writing is the best way to reading, for which there is little evidence. Widdowson (1978) does, however, make the point that both writing and reading can be taught together with mutual benefit in an 'integrated skills' approach. A constructive exercise used frequently for teaching initial L_1 reading is the 'language experience' approach: the child tells a story, the teacher notes it down as told, and the child then reads it. Its use in the L_2 should raise no greater problems of accuracy or style than it does in L_1. Another type of exercise, which tends to develop sensitivity to chronological sequence markers and other indicators of cohesion, is Moody's (1976) multiple choice completion task. In this, students read the first sentence of the passage, then have to choose the best candidate for the second from three plausible completions, the third from another set of three, and so on. The following exercise is based on Moody's principle.

From the alternatives (a) (b) and (c) select the sentence which would best continue the numbered passage:

(1) *Tony Smith lived with his mother in Duke Street. He liked a life of routine.*
   (a) *Mrs Smith was a housewife.*
   (b) *Duke Street is a long, straight road with small houses on either side.*
   (c) *Every day he went to work by car, parking it in the underground car park.*

(2) *Tony Smith lived with his mother in Duke Street. He liked a life of routine. Every day he went to work by car, parking it in the underground car park.*
   (a) *On Fridays he left work early to take his mother to the shops.*
   (b) *Suddenly he bought a new one.*
   (c) *It was a wide expanse of concrete reached by a steep ramp.*

(3) *Tony Smith lived with his mother in Duke Street. He liked a life of routine. Every day he went to work by car, parking it in the underground car park. On Fridays he left work early to take his mother to the shops.*
   (a) *His mother was Mrs Smith.*
   (b) *However, on this particular Friday, she did not go to the shops with him.*
   (c) *At this moment, he is leaving work early.*
(And so on.)

A third type of constructive approach is the set of exercises called by Widdowson (1978) 'gradual approximation'. In this, reading the whole text is the endpoint of a graded series of simpler exercises designed to lead to a full understanding of the text. The basis of the exercises is analysis of the text into all its component propositions, out of which are developed exercises in vocabulary choice, sentence reordering, grammatical transformation, sentence synthesis and the conversion of information into picture or diagram form.

These two sections on comprehension have leaned heavily on the notion of heuristic strategies for integrating spoken or written text and exercise types which claim to foster the development of such strategies for all L_2 communication. This does not imply that the student might not already be using these strategies in the first language; the problem for the L_2 teacher is to help him/her use them in L_2.

Production of Language

Compared to the sections on comprehension, this section on language production will be rather short. This is for two reasons. One is simply that, in fact, not a great deal is known about cognitive processes in producing utterances. There has been greater progress in the study of comprehension. The other is that some of the most interesting work in teaching spoken and to some extent written language is based on social-psychological considerations, such as group dynamics and interpersonal communications, and will therefore be discussed in the chapter devoted to social factors.

At the beginning of this chapter two ways of teaching the passive voice in English were compared and the point made that neither of them appeared to be based on psychologically real processes. In general, the popular transformation exercise, based on structural grammar, depends on the notion that sentences are altered versions of other sentences. If this was really the way we plan and produce utterances it would seem to be a highly wasteful procedure; there is no evidence to support it and quite a lot against it. Such exercises are only knowledge games; they increase the students' facility at structural manipulation, and thereby help him/her to internalise grammatical rules of various kinds, but they do not relate to actual processes in production of language.

Nevertheless, speakers and writers do have to choose syntactic structure for their utterances, as well as much other structure. Clark and Clark (1977) give a useful five-stage description of the stages in planning and producing an utterance, which indicates the complexity of the process that native speakers take so much for granted:

Discourse plans

Speakers select appropriate plans for different speech activities and acts: telling stories, giving instructions, persuading others, describing things, and so on. These plans may refer to long stretches of language, such as the organisation of a story, and short stretches, such as the appropriate phrase for obtaining obedience given a particular social situation.

Sentence plans

Particular syntactic forms are chosen which realise the plans decided above; in other words, the actual packaging or staging of the message to conform to those decisions – in terms of subordination, information focus, topicalisation, and so on.

Constituent plans

Individual constituents, that is, noun phrases, verb phrases, tone groups, are filled out with particular words.

Articulatory plans

A running memory of the phonological shape of the utterance, with all the intended words, inflections, stresses and intonation.

Articulation

The articulatory plan is executed by translating the phonological shape into actual movements of the articulators.

In speech it is relatively rare that this complex process is able to proceed fluently and without hitch unless it has been rehearsed in some way. Most normal native speech has a relatively high incidence of errors: changes of mind, backtracking, reformulations, and less than optimal word choice. It is not surprising, therefore, that both speaking and writing are regarded as difficult skills which not all native speakers attain to the same degree. One must be careful not to demand higher standards from L_2 learners than one does from native speakers.

Evidence for these stages of planning comes mainly from naturalistic study of hesitations, pauses and speech errors, which in this context can be likened to Goodman's miscues in reading. Speech errors are not random; there are a certain number of frequently occurring types; and they permit certain generalisations. For example, it seems likely that transposition errors (an/a:/s/i/b/l/ay/s/t/ for *an icy blast*) only occur with constituents and not across their boundaries, thus indicating that the constituent is a unit of phonological planning. Fromkin (1973) analysed a reversal error (someone saying *a maniac for weekends* for *a weekend for maniacs*) and found that that particular error, which preserved the stress pattern of the original intended phrase, could have been produced by a set of plans such as those outlined above going wrong at the word-selection stage, and selecting the two words required but putting them into the wrong slots.

Non-native speakers naturally are more likely to fall into these kinds of planning and execution traps in speech. It is not uncommon for the intended message simply to overload the learner's planning capacity and for him/her to give up and say something simpler. This can be immensely frustrating, particularly for an adult who wishes to be recognised as the intelligent human being he/she sounds like in the native tongue.

However, the number of teaching techniques that are available to ease this problem are rather few. Clearly, conversation with a sympathetic listener is a possible, though unstructured and expensive, solution. It is not clear how effective little fluency practice exercises, like quick prompt drills, are, though their use is widespread, for example:

> The cats are in the garden
> lions   The lions are in the garden
> park   The lions are in the park.

This one is aimed only at the stage in the process where constituents are filled out with actual words; although if we are to believe the above explanation of speech errors, it is constituents with skeleton meanings, technically lists of semantic features, which are completed with appropriate lexical items. Many experienced language learners (Pickett, 1978) have reported that they derived no perceptible benefit from structural and other types of practice, and that the only useful preparation for normal communicative use of language was not separate exercises for particular operations, but holistic attempts at normal conversational fluency. We take up this theme again in the chapter on second language learning research and in discussing social factors.

Summary

This chapter has reviewed some possible relationships between grammars and psychological processes, investigated comprehension strategies and exercise types to encourage their development and looked at speech planning and some questions associated with its pedagogy.

Chapter 5

Memory

There are many reasons why teachers of all subjects are interested in memory and forgetting. Pupils sometimes seem to need large amounts of practice on some point before it will be remembered, at other times a single mention is sufficient. Some pupils appear to need constant reminders about some piece of necessary information, others learn it seemingly without effort. There are wide differences, then, between the memory demands of different tasks and between individuals' memory abilities. For the language teacher there are also different goals, concerning long-term and short-term objectives. Usually these are consonant, as when a new structural pattern is introduced which is to be remembered and placed in its context in the learner's growing store of syntactic devices that are legal in the new language. Sometimes, however, the goals may be mildly in conflict, as when a new word is introduced and one of its senses explained, but in the long term it has to be understood in a variety of senses, for none of which there is an exact translation equivalent.

'Memory' means many things to many people. To the psychologist, it is an area of research which spans concern for the mechanisms of retention of information for periods of less than half a second, through the organisation of our store of knowledge about the world, ourselves, our language(s), and other people, to the breakdown of this store and its attendant processes of intake and retrieval in amnesia (loss of memory) and other pathological states such as aphasia (loss of speech). Some idea of the range of interrelating studies which research into memory has produced can be seen in Figure 5.1.

As can be seen, studies of memory are not restricted to the relatively simple situation of memorising facts and figures, but extend into the development, nature, and pathology of the processes by which everything we know, including our language, is assimilated and kept available for use.

It was assumed for many years that human memory was something like a tablet of wax upon which an accurate impression was made by experience; and forgetting was due to the gradual erosion of the sharp

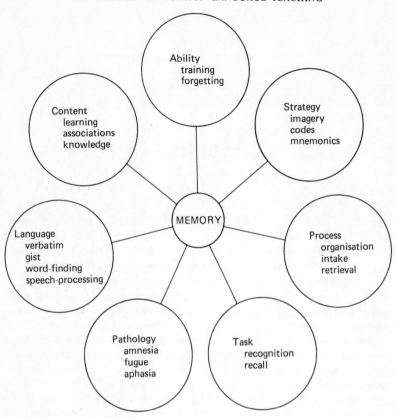

Figure 5.1 *Topics associated with memory.*

contours of the image. A more up-to-date analogy, with the same import, would be a tape recording. Many experiments have shown this view to be incorrect, but it is not difficult to see that such a view must be wrong on logical grounds. If we preserved a totally accurate record of experience, from which the only playback was in the exact order of the original events, there would be no possibility of comparing events, selecting and grouping experiences for different purposes and producing novel solutions to problems requiring previous knowledge. This would be because of two reasons: first, the sheer amount of material to be reviewed and secondly, the restriction to the original order of events. It is therefore biologically adaptive to have a memory system which is selective and capable of reorganising information for new uses, although there is naturally a cost in terms of the possibilities of forgetting.

Structure and organisation

In this section we will investigate some of the distinctions drawn by psychologists in the attempt to specify the limitations and nature of memory processes and relate them to various aspects of language and language learning. The distinctions that have been found necessary fall into three basic categories: time, process and type of information. Much of the discussion will recall the arguments presented in Chapters 2 and 3 about behaviouristic or associationist approaches to learning and information-processing ones. In particular, the discussion of explanations of memory in terms of frequency of exposure and repetition of items will recall behaviourist claims about response strength, and discussion of internal organisation, subjective categorisation and response biases will recall the information-processing approach. Modern advances in the study of memory and forgetting have almost exclusively been promoted by information-processing theory and not a little by models of computer memories.

Distinctions by time

Frequently, we are able to recall information for immediate use that we cannot recall after some delay in time. For example, if we look up a telephone number we did not previously know it is not difficult to retain it for immediate dialling, but if we have to dial again after a few moments it is often necessary to consult the directory again. It is also possible to learn a telephone number by heart and this requires extra work of various kinds. The distinction may be seen in the language classroom in the student who can recall a new word or phrase immediately after it has been discussed by the teacher or the class, but who cannot recall it after the class unless specific kinds of extra work are demanded. A great deal of study has been devoted to this distinction between immediate, or short-term, memory and long-term memory. Several facts are well known; immediate memory has a relatively small capacity and information in it lasts only a short time, so that the longer the telephone number, the more errors and the longer the delay, the more is forgotten. One way of investigating the span of immediate memory is to present a series of unconnected objects, words or pictures at a steady rate and ask for immediate recall of them; in these conditions, people can recall correctly if the series contains around seven items, but if it contains more, some are lost. If the series contains many more than this, let us say fifteen or twenty independent items, the pattern of forgetting is characteristic and instructive. Recall depends on the position of the item in the list: early items and late items are recalled best but those in the middle are forgotten. This may be seen in Figure 5.2.

This effect, which is very stable and can happen, for instance, when a student is learning an uncontextualised vocabulary list, is usually taken as evidence for the short-term/long-term distinction. Success with the last

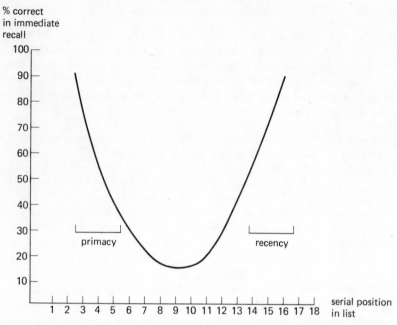

Figure 5.2   *An illustrative serial position curve for immediate free recall.*

items, the 'recency' effect, demonstrates immediate memory and is remarkably stable, disappearing only when there is an enforced delay in recall (that is, when recall is not immediate). Success on the early items, the 'primacy' effect, is attributed to the extra work the person has had to perform on them to retain them (whether cumulative rehearsal, grouping, inventing associations, or using a mnemonic) and is affected by all the influences that can affect our long-term store of information.

A distinction has conventionally been drawn, then, on the basis of evidence such as this, between immediate and long-term memory and the inference made that the distinction in time reflects a difference in type of storage or process. Here, the one task appears to engage two types of memory store or process and this is typical of most memory tasks. There are very few which do not involve both. If we accept this distinction, at least for items that have no apparent connection with each other, like lists of nonsense syllables, unconnected names of objects, digits, and so on, we can ask if the language they are presented in makes any difference to the capacity of immediate memory. Lado (1965) discovered that the memory span for digits (the number correctly recalled immediately after presentation) was slightly smaller for a group of native English speakers in the language they were learning, Spanish, than in English, but attributed it to the greater number of syllables in the Spanish words. Cook (1977) also investigated this matter and found that there was hardly any difference in capacity for digits in the foreign language, but there was for other types of words, like object names. This may have been because there is only a small set of single digit names and they are therefore easier for a non-native speaker to recognise than object names, which require information from deeper in the long-term memory. However, this implies more subtle distinctions in memory than the simple one of time and it is to these we now turn.

Distinctions by process

Chunking It has been known since the last century that the capacity of immediate memory is limited, but it is only comparatively recently that the significance of that limited capacity has been recognised. G. A. Miller (1956) showed that the limitation was approximately seven items, however complex those items were and from whatever number of possible similar items they were chosen. That is to say, the limitation was in terms of perceptible chunks of information, rather than on the information itself. Thus the limitation remained roughly constant whether the material stored was simple abstract designs, letters, simple sounds, syllables, or unconnected words. This is in quite marked contrast to long-term memory, in which the amount recalled, the time it is retained and the errors in recall depend largely on factors inherent in the structure and organisation of the particular material and in the types of coding performed on it.

Working memory Before looking at some of the processes affecting long-term recall mention must be made of the concept of 'working memory' or 'speech-processing memory' which was used in the previous chapter. Most of the work on short-term memory discussed so far involved people recalling lists or arrays of independent items. As soon as there is any connection between the items, whether real or imagined, such as physical grouping, similarity of sound or meaning, rhythmic presentation, or grammatical structure, there exists redundant information and this can be used to circumvent the otherwise rather severe limitations. The question naturally arises as to whether these restrictions operate when the material to be remembered is connected discourse, or whether quite other processes intervene. In the last chapter it was mentioned that the first stage of the process of interpreting spoken text is a short-term phonological store with severe restrictions, according to some authorities the capacity for one clause, according to others the capacity for one tone group, or complete speech melody. How these restrictions on connected discourse relate to those on chunks of information is not clear at present. However, it is plain that there must be some kind of short-term storage for linguistic material and since it is rather severely limited, the problem for both native and non-native speakers of the language is to extract the important information from it by calling up the necessary knowledge from long-term storage and applying interpretive processes as quickly as possible. Rivers (1971) made some practical suggestions for exercises to enlarge the working memory capacity in the second language by practising rhythmic, intonational and syntactic groupings in rapid repetition of a model; these have not been empirically tested. The benefit they might provide is probably in the increased ease of calling up previously stored linguistic information, in other words, using the long-term memory component rather than, as it were, increasing the space available.

Frequency   Long-term memory was first studied on a large experimental scale by Ebbinghaus, who, in his *Über das Gedächtnis* (1885) reported a long series of experiments on his own learning of lists of deliberately meaningless items. The material he used was nonsense syllables, which he defended by arguing that real words held too much inherent variability of association for any general conclusions to be drawn about memory *per se*, rather than about idiosyncracies of the contents of memory. One of his methods was known as the method of 'saving'. In this method, he would repeatedly read a list to himself until he could recall it to a certain criterion level, say, twice perfectly, and repeat the whole process at certain intervals, say, daily or weekly. By counting the number of rehearsals necessary at each session, he could plot a learning curve which showed the saving of

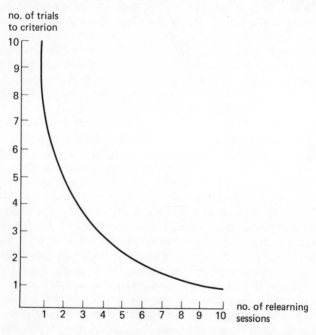

Figure 5.3   *An illustrative learning curve using the saving method.*

time in relearning at each successive learning session. See Figure 5.3.

Typically, such a learning curve would show a fairly rapid improvement followed by a long period of slow mastery. This type of experiment gives the flavour of Ebbinghaus's arduous and lonely task and also shows that despite the undoubted artificiality of the nonsense syllables, some of the properties of a long-term memory could be revealed by the method, in particular its response to frequency of presentation.

Any foreign language learner dealing with a new word (which is at first little more than a nonsense syllable to him, after all) needs to encounter that word frequently, perhaps in different contexts as long as the sense is identical, either by voluntary search or by involuntary discovery in texts and exercises. At each encounter the saving of time in recognition or relearning (which can be equated here) will increase and Ebbinghaus's learning curve can be seen operating.

The influence of frequency of presentation or encounter on retention cannot be denied, but it can be overemphasised. Ebbinghaus and his methods have been heavily criticised, not least by Bartlett (1932), who argued that nonsense syllables were never actually meaningless (for example, YUQ, ZIG, GOL) and that people may make much odder and more variable associations to them than to common language with its conventional meaning. Bartlett also claimed that by ignoring the 'conditions of response which belong to the subjective attitude and to predetermined reaction tendencies' Ebbinghaus was failing to account for possibly more important features of memory. The effort to rid stimuli of meaning was likely to make memory studies merely 'a study of the establishment and maintenance of repetition habits' (1932, p. 4). Unfortunately, for another decade or two after Bartlett's attack, a large proportion of the work on memory became just that. Some of Bartlett's own work on memory organisation will be taken up later.

Associative clusters   The influences of pre-existing knowledge stored in long-term memory on an immediate recall task was demonstrated some time ago by Bousfield (1953). He showed that subjects could recall many more words than the classical memory span of approximately seven items when the words could be grouped into clusters which had some unifying feature. Thus a list made up of four words each describing sports, metals, foods, birds and cars, in a jumbled or random order, might be as easily recalled as a six-item list of independent items, although twenty items would normally be beyond memory span. This effect of 'associative clustering' indicated that one of the contributions of long-term memory to short-term memory was knowledge about how words and concepts were associated together. Bousfield originally interpreted this finding in terms of word associations, but later researchers showed that the most significant influence was the organisation of words together as labels for various semantic categories; and the next decade saw a large amount of work in verbal learning devoted to discovering the principal ways in which the organisation of words, concepts and categories affected various memory tasks.

The work on associative clustering and categorial recall holds strong implications for language teaching and learning. The need for frequency of encounter for a saving in learning effort was shown in the previous section; just as important is the need for the integration of new vocabulary items into organised clusters or categories. Naturally the first language will provide much of the organising framework, but learning new words by translation equivalents alone is notoriously misleading. Even where familiar concepts are concerned, for which there is a full set of terms in the first language, new vocabulary items in the second language need to be placed in a framework which is faithful to the aspects of meaning coded in the new language. That is to say, new vocabulary items should be introduced in relation to other L_2 items within the same field of meaning or cluster, so that necessary meaning relations, that is, membership of a category, category label, opposites, complements, and so on, can be appreciated and used as aids to recall.

Codes   Recall is influenced by events or processes at various stages of memory. Three stages can conveniently be distinguished: intake, storage and retrieval. The manner and type of storage of information is possibly the most interesting of these, since it is essentially a question of the mental representation of all our knowledge. Some attempts to investigate this representation will be reviewed later in the chapter. However, the manner of intake of information – the type of memory code assigned to it, the organisation of it recognised or imposed by the learner – has a great effect on subsequent retention, as can be seen in a simple, but perhaps surprising, experiment of Tulving's (1966).

He asked two groups of people to learn a nine-word list followed by an eighteen-word list. For one group, the eighteen-word list contained the nine words already learned, that is, there were only nine new words. One might expect, on grounds of frequency of exposure, that the group with only nine new words to learn would perform better in the second task. In fact, the other group, who had eighteen new words to learn and had learned nine irrelevant words first, performed better overall on the second task. Presumably the codings the groups assigned to the nine-word list (probably associations, a story, or a mnemonic of some sort) hindered the learning of the nine new words for the first group, but was simply irrelevant for the group learning eighteen all-new words. Thus even in short-term memory tasks forgetting can be due to the type of coding employed at intake.

It is not always easy to separate influences of coding at intake from influences of the use of words in retrieval. One illustration of retrieval failure is Tulving and Pearlstone's (1966) demonstration of the difference between what is available for recall and what is actually accessible. Their subjects learnt lists of forty-eight words, which consisted of four words from each of twelve categories and the category names were announced before each group of words (for example: animals -- lion, elephant, tiger, baboon; trees -- oak, elm, plane, sycamore; vegetables -- leek, carrot, cabbage, potato, and so on). Typically, people can recall two or three from each category remembered, but some whole categories are forgotten. However, if the names of the missing categories are given as prompts afterwards, they can recall words from these categories. Thus more information is available for recall than is actually accessible at the time. In this case, retrieval was aided by repetition of the original category names as prompts for a memory search; in teaching, it is often possible to assume that something has not been learnt by a student when in fact it is available but needs extra questioning, and in the long term the development of memory search strategies, to make it accessible. The problem is often compounded when students are asked to recall words and other information in a context which is different from that of the original learning. This requires a flexibility of subjective organisation achieved through different encounters with the information in question and the development of a variety of links between the new information and existing knowledge.

There have been several suggestions for types of codes to act as recall aids in foreign language learning. Two will be mentioned here. Stevick (1976) attributes to Curran a technique for remembering foreign vocabulary which uses what psychologists called 'natural language mediators' and which Curran calls 'security words'. A mediator, in this sense, is a third word which is learnt in association with a pair of words, and which provides a link from one to the other. In Curran's technique for learning pairs of translation equivalents, a word is found from the L_1 which shares both an acoustic similarity with the L_2 word to be learned, and a semantic feature with both members of the pair. Thus, in learning the pair

$$chorny \text{ (Russian)} = black \text{ (English)}$$

the mediator *charred* might be pointed out to or discovered by the students. An example from a non-Indo-European language might be

$$göz \text{ (Turkish)} = eye \text{ (English)}$$

using the mediator *gaze*. This sort of imposed coding by links with other convenient words may be quite useful, especially in the early stages when there are few L_2 words available as a framework. There are two obvious dangers if it is used indiscriminately. First, the mediator may be too well learned and recalled as the L_1 equivalent itself rather than simply a link with the true equivalent. Secondly, and this is a danger with all vocabulary learning that treats words as single units, large numbers of sound shapes have several meanings. Thus *charred*, if spelled *chard* refers to a green vegetable somewhat like spinach, which is not going to help recall the word *black*.

The second coding technique employs a simple mediational principle but uses a picture or a mental image instead of a third word. Ott and his colleagues (1973) have experimented with images which capitalise on acoustic similarities between words in the two languages. One of their examples is the pair

eye (English) = *Auge* (German)

They recommend the drawing, either by the teacher or by the pupil, of an image which suggests that equivalence both directly and indirectly via the association

egg (English) = *Ei* (German)

See Figure 5.4.

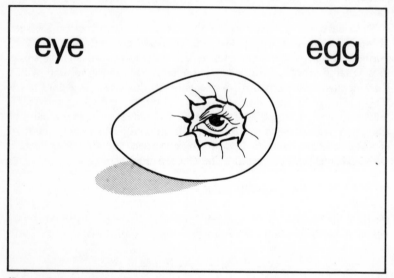

(Source: Ott *et al.*, 1973, p. 99, fig. 1.)

Figure 5.4   *An Interactive Picture for the German word* Ei

Of course, there are not very many pairs of words for which this technique could be used, even using languages as closely related as German and English. Ott *et al.* claim that this 'elaboration of an interactive image' aided school pupils to a significant extent in learning German vocabulary. This illustrates in quite a dramatic way the use of codings in intake and retrieval; but we can ask whether the improvement in performance in their experiment was actually due to the visual image, or to the language mediators it was based on, or merely to the fact that the students were being asked to do a novel and quite amusing, but different, vocabulary learning task. Studies of visual imagery have always had to face the problem of whether effects of imagery in memory are real or only apparent. However vivid the image is to the experiencer, recall performance may in fact only depend on the linguistic and acoustic links thereby symbolised.

Schemas   So far, mention has been made only of relatively superficial types and effects of subjective organisation. However, perhaps the most striking demonstration of this concerns memory for the contents of longish passages of fact and fiction, like stories, reports and talks. It was studies of this type of memory that led Bartlett to reject as vacuous the explanations of memory in terms of frequency. He showed that the kinds of alterations that creep into passages, particularly stories, recalled repeatedly by one person, or passed orally along a chain of people, are not random but exhibit considerable systematicity. For example, certain details are sharpened (for example, 'warriors' faces' in the original might become 'fierce warriors' faces'), some are levelled, or omitted, and some are rationalised (for example, an unusual or baffling motivation for some action might be replaced by a more familiar one). He also noted 'the curious tendency to preserve the apparently odd, trivial, disconnected and novel element' (1932, p. 273). Bartlett saw in these systematic alterations, omissions, transpositions and rationalisations, the operation of a schema, indeed of several, which related the story or passage heard to previously existing expectations of what might have occurred. Recall, for him, was a constructive or reconstructive process. The retelling of a story was the result of the story being constructed anew from the traces of the first hearing guided by schemata of expectations about possible occurrences, possible motivations, settings, characters and story conventions.

There are also many ways individual recallers differ. One that has received some study (Holzman and Gardner, 1960) is that tendency towards either levelling or sharpening of details in recall; people who level out details also group other objects together, or assimilate them, to an extent that sharpeners are reluctant to. In Holzman and Gardner's study of the recall of the Pied Piper story, the sharpeners were also the most accurate rememberers.

An obvious difficulty with the schema concept is that it is too vague. Recently, however, psychologists working with language have brought the schema idea up to date with modern computer technology and have developed rather more precise descriptions. The sort of facts they seek to account for are the alterations in memory noticed by Bartlett, the ways in which some points are subsumed into others, details are forgotten and give way to main points, and the whole reduced to a gist which preserves the main skeleton of the meaning from which, perhaps, some of the detailed arguments and points of example can be recovered. A synopsis of modern work will be found in Bower's (1976) lecture in honour of Sir Frederick Bartlett.

The precise details of this modern work, which entail the mathematics of formal grammar, are not important for language teaching purposes. The two important points to note from this type of study are the constructive nature of recall and the problem of contextualisation of exercises and drills. The phrase 'constructive nature of recall' will itself recall the concern of the previous chapter for the constructive nature of the process of comprehension. This parallel between the active, if unconscious, processes of comprehension and the act of recall is not fortuitous. The domains of memory and comprehension are not clear cut; the interaction between them is considerable. Neisser (1967) puts the point neatly:

> one does not recall objects or responses simply because traces of them exist in the mind, but after an elaborate process of *re*construction, which usually makes use of relevant stored information.
>
> What is the information ... on which reconstruction is based? The only plausible possibility is that it consists of traces of *prior processes of construction*. (p. 285)

The problem, in a language teaching context, is how to give the students sufficient directed opportunity to reconstruct and revive meanings and material given in the foreign language. This is, of course, one possible justification for the present trend towards integrated skills, in which a theme is exploited using spoken and written material, reading, listening and discussion skills.

The problem of contextualisation of skills and exercises is in some ways related to that above; but here the question is essentially whether a language point presented in the context of a little story is easier or less easy to assimilate and understand than if presented in a drill with items connected only by the recurrence of that language form. Compare, for example:

(a) *The boy slipped on the banana because he did not look where he was going.*
He hurt his leg because he slipped on the banana.
He was taken to hospital because he hurt his leg.
He had a day off school because he was in hospital.
He missed an English lesson because he had a day off school.

(and so on)

(b) *The girl bought a hat because she liked it.*
The man drove to London because the trains were on strike.

The teacher encouraged the pupil because his work was good.
The boy ran to school because he missed the bus.

(and so on)

Exercise (a) forms a little, highly concocted story; exercise (b) contains topically unconnected items. It has been argued (Oller and Obrecht, 1969) that exercises are best assimilated if the information in them follows a recognisable and familiar sequence. Their idea of the 'psycholinguistic principle of information sequence' appears to be no more than the use of some conventional schema, of which a chronological sequence, or story, is just one kind. In other words, the contextualised drill claims that repetition of a form in a coherent context promotes learning better than repetition of that form without the context. There is another interpretation of contextualisation which recalls the discussion of analytic, or holist, approaches on pp. 75 ff. In this, a context, perhaps a typical everyday situation or a dramatised occasion for some particular language notion or function, serves as the link between a heterogeneous collection of language forms whose interrelations are demonstrated by the context. They may be different things one might wish to say in that situation, or different ways of expressing the same thing.

In exercise (a) a story consisting of the maximum number of cause and effect relations is an obvious device for teaching *because*; it also allows a certain amount of prediction and the creation of phrases and continuation of the chain by the students. However, it is a very weak story precisely because it only exploits one type of narrative episode; in long-term recall this might lead to skipping of steps, and this, though unimportant here, might be undesirable in other contexts. Schemas for stories are usually more complicated, containing settings, developments, episodes and resolutions. Therefore designing contextualised exercises necessarily involves a compromise between transparency or clarity in the presentation of the actual teaching point and naturalness of the story chosen as the context.

Distinctions by type of material

Up till now we have spoken as if all the material we retain is of the same kind, and as if therefore our representation of it is, in principle, similar. However, an important distinction was drawn by Tulving (1972) between episodic and semantic memory. Essentially, episodic memory refers to stored information that is coded by chronology: (auto)biographical details, sequences of events, what X said when he was drinking his coffee, the list of appointments for the day, and so on. Tulving also pointed out that large numbers of experiments on verbal memory also fell into this category, especially when dealing with particular occurrences of words in certain orders in lists. He contrasted this with the kind of memory we have for the sounds, rules, words and meanings of our language, which is quite divorced from the original occasion or setting of our learning or encountering them, and is available for any purpose. This is semantic memory. It is important to note, therefore, that any learning technique or memory coding system must allow the language information to lose the episodic characteristics it has at first and be absorbed into the general system of semantic memory.

A great deal of effort is now being devoted to the study of the organisation of this type of information, concerned with the mental representation of words and their meanings, of the concepts which make up the raw material of our thoughts and the words we can express them by. It is customary to divide the problem into the question of mental lexicons or cerebral dictionaries, that is, the ways in which words and their possible interrelationships are stored, and mental encyclopedias, the ways in which concepts are stored, and the type of indexing that must exist between the two. These problems are remarkably complicated in the case of the monolingual; but the presence of two or more languages implies added complications. The languages can be kept separate, but translations can be found; many bilinguals also have concepts which are unique to their experience of one of the languages. There must therefore be some sort of common storage, which nevertheless allows discrimination between the languages, for most bilinguals can keep to one or other language fairly consistently in production; and yet there also exists some unique storage for each language. Research into bilingual semantic memory has concentrated on the problem of the integrity of the language systems – whether the words, for example, of each language are stored separately or together – and the relationship between the languages and the underlying conceptual system they can be used to express.

Some researchers have used the bilingual's ability to switch between languages as a technique for investigating the first question. Kolers (1966) found that bilinguals took longer to read aloud texts which mixed the languages than texts in either language. Taylor (1971) used word association – giving a word and asking for the first word that occurs to the subject – in several conditions of switching, and found that bilinguals found it easier, and preferred, making associations within one language to making associations across languages. These results suggest that the languages are organised as rather separate systems. But other investigators, for example, Neufeld (1976) also using a switching task, have found contradictory results. Of course, it is perfectly possible that the words of each of the bilingual's languages are stored with the strongest associative links between words of the same language but with weaker links between the different languages. Kintsch and Kintsch (1969) investigated the phenomenon that many bilinguals report, that of finding difficulty in remembering which language a message had been in. They gave a simple paired-associate learning task. The bilinguals learned two lists. In one, there were four German words and four English translation equivalents, paired with the digits one to eight. In the other list, there were four German words and four unrelated English words, paired with the digits. In a way which recalls Tulving's experiment on subjective organisation at intake, the first list required the subjects to learn new meanings on only half the number of items. Nevertheless, it was this list that was the most difficult to recall, because remembering which language a word had been in is much more difficult when it is the crucial cue than when it is part of a unique language-meaning pair. Therefore, bilinguals can code words either in terms of meaning or terms of which language they belong to, according to the demands of the task, but cannot separate the two types of information completely. This should not be surprising, since it is rare for any words to have exact translation equivalents in other languages, and an important aspect of the meaning of any word is the way it is distinct from the other words describing the same field or referent in the same language.

Some Pedagogical Problems

In conclusion, we shall see how this rather complex picture of memory for language informs some specific language teaching problems.

Learning by rote

This has been a favourite technique in some quarters for years. There is no doubt that in the early stages of learning a foreign language, the ability to perform a rote-learned chunk in the foreign language has some motivational advantage; it gives a sense of achievement not necessarily dimmed by the perception that not all the internal relationships in the material are fully understood. It is also a useful party piece to gain parental encouragement. But, in general, the picture of human memory outlined above shows it to be rather irrelevant to the complex task of gradually building up a representation in semantic memory of the new language code, in a form which is flexible and usable in novel ways in novel contexts. Melvin and Rivers (1976) make a similar point, from the point of view of theories of computer memory, in distinguishing between 'learning' and 'memorisation'.

There is one exception to this negative judgement, which is the use made by L_2 learners of 'prefabricated patterns' (Hakuta, 1976), to stand for complex grammatical phrases they have not yet mastered. These are, in a sense, grammatical strings of words learned by rote and not constructed by rule, which enable communication to take place, and which gradually break down and become invested with grammatical insight.

Strategies for learning and retrieval

Another implication which seems to be clear from the above picture is that the teacher's task is not so much to arrange for repetition or recycling of L_2 vocabulary, phrases, or structural patterns, but to help the student discover strategies for organising his or her own knowledge, whether into semantic or associative clusters as in the Bousfield experiments, or 'meaning hierarchies'. Of course, the conceptual system the learner has acquired with and through the first language is bound to be both a blessing and a burden in this process, and for this reason learners often manage to retain some of the episodic information surrounding new L_2 words, to link it with the original learning situation. Here speaks an anonymous contributor to Pickett's (1978) retrospective data on foreign language learning:

> I never found learning lists of words the arid task it sounds but it [language] has always evoked [situation] best for me when the words are organised into topics or when the vocabulary list is a personal evocative reminder of the situation it was garnered in, as, for example, the booklets I brought back with me from a term spent at a German University where the words were a highly personalised diary, e.g. why wood sorrel? Because we made punch requiring the addition of this. (Pickett, 1978, p. 97, contributor M)

Teachers who are unable to provide this sort of local colour can nevertheless encourage their students to make their own vocabulary demands with silent film, slides and other visual material, and more informal classroom activities. Even the humdrum process of presenting or exploiting the unfamiliar words and phrases in a reading comprehension text can be used as the basis of the development of such strategies by the student, by organising the unfamiliar items in different ways: in the order they appear, as a lexical skeleton of the passage; grouped by semantic category; and grouped by association with other known words of close meaning.

The role of comprehension questions

It is a truism to point out that the technique of asking questions after a reading or a listening task is a testing technique and not a teaching technique. Students are assumed to comprehend and learn by unanalysed processes and the teacher checks that they have done the work. As a testing technique, however, there are many problems concerning the form of the questions, the role of errors originating from the production of the answer; the difficulty of the language of the questions. Two other, perhaps less tractable, problems with comprehension questions as testing devices give a clue to a possible teaching function. They concern the tendency of test-like questions to suggest their own answers. The first problem is the unfortunate tendency of people to believe in the reasonableness of the question and select an answer according to it, rather than to their original perception of the text. This appears dramatically in a quite different context as the problem of 'leading questions' in the recall of witnesses in legal cases. Questions can be asked in such a way that the answer is biased away from the original perception of the event, which may of course have been fleeting or vague. Loftus (1975) has shown how witnesses' recall can be subtly influenced by the form of the questions. In one of her studies, a film of a car accident was shown. The question 'About how fast were the cars going when they smashed into each other?' consistently yielded a higher estimate of speed than when the words 'collided', 'bumped', 'contacted', or 'hit' were used. Thus the wording of questions given immediately after an event can influence the mental representation quite considerably, probably by some kind of social pressure to conform to the implied opinion of an authority figure.

The second problem concerns the extent to which, in a series of questions, the wording of some gives the answers to others. One of the simplest tests for the validity of a set of comprehension questions in a language test is whether they can be answered correctly without having read the passage.

Naturally, both these problems with test items also affect the use of comprehension questions as teaching devices. If the student can work out answers without reading the passage, he will not learn how to read passages. Nevertheless, these problems can be seen as negative but controllable aspects of an important principle, which is related to the previous discussion about recall as reconstruction. Our mental representation, or memory schema, for an experience, under which we can include linguistic texts, is not a static thing but a dynamic one, changing with reflection, comparison with other information and subsequent events such as questions. As described in Chapter 4 (pp. 53–4), Rothkopf (1970) and Frase (1972) have performed extensive experiments on learning from textual materials with various types of test-like events. They conclude that type and position of questions (before, during, or after the text) heavily influence the amount and nature of the information from the text retained in long-term memory. McDonough (1976) reports a small-scale experiment in second language learning concerned with this difference between the 'tapping' and 'guiding' functions of questions.

The model of memory that all such conceptions of teaching activities are based upon is thus a dynamic, constructive one. The pedagogic problem becomes one of evaluating whether comprehension questions (pre-text, interspersed, or post-text is here immaterial) are suitable for training the particular subskill intended and, if it is decided affirmatively, what kinds of questions are productive and what kinds are counterproductive. Some of the alternatives to questions were described in Chapter 4. As part of the answer (but only a part) to the supplementary problem, one might wish to distinguish between questions whose answers are simply constituents of particular sentences, and questions whose answers require inferences between constituents and across sentence boundaries. For example:

Jim rode past on a horse. Blood was streaming from the animal's flank.

(1) Who rode past?
(2) What did he ride on?
(3) What did Jim do?
(4) Which animal was bleeding?
(5) What might have caused the bleeding?

The first three of these simple questions could be answered by single constituents, and might indeed be answered simply by repetitions of the first sentence; the fourth and fifth require inference and speculation respectively.

Summary

In this chapter we have looked at various subdivisions of the concept of memory and related them to various problems in the teaching of languages. In general, an organisational, constructive view of memory has been preferred over a view based on frequency and repetition, and implications from such a view for language teaching and testing have been considered.

Chapter 6

Social and Interpersonal Factors

The previous chapters have been largely concerned with cognitive and behavioural factors within the individual. We have looked briefly at cognitive processes, comprehension of language, the building of habits and memory organisation. But rarely are learners totally isolated, without contact with other learners, and rarely are they learning without actual or expected contact with speakers of the language, either in person or in writing. It is therefore time to look at the social-psychological effects on the learner of learning a new medium of communication, and of being a member of a learning group. It is convenient, therefore, to distinguish between social factors in the eventual communication situation for which the language is being learned, which might influence the choice of language knowledge and skills to be taught, and social factors in the learning situation itself, which may be, desirably or undesirably, an important part of the learning process.

It is a commonplace that most language classrooms are artificial and one sense of this term (non-genuineness) implies that these two types of social factor are widely separated, that is to say that the classroom does not reflect the eventual language-using situation. For this reason there has been for some time a trend towards a greater degree of realism in the classroom, in terms of the language items included, the types of activities allowed, and the kinds of interaction between people provoked. But such moves, however welcome, do not remove the artificiality of the classroom in the slightly different sense of artificial, meaning 'made by hand'. It is still the teacher's responsibility to plan and execute the appropriate classroom organisation and activities and monitor their success as reflected in the students' improvement. This chapter examines some of the social-psychological factors the teacher has to take account of, with illustrations of some types of exercise, and ends with a brief consideration of the wider social concerns which may indirectly affect the students' success.

Language Skills as Social Skills

Most of the discussion in the earlier chapters has been concerned with learning in the sense of the acquisition of knowledge of various kinds. However, language teaching is primarily concerned with the training of language skills: to 'speak a language like a native' means to be able to do all the things with the language that a native speaker can do, and if that aim is unreasonably high for second language learners, then their objectives are usually a more or less limited set of the things that native speakers, perhaps only in some specified circumstances, can and do do with their language. (In fact in many parts of the world English is learned for communicating primarily with other non-native speakers of it; for the present argument we can group these proficient L_2 speakers with native speakers as a reference group.) In general, second language learners are gaining mastery over the language used by native speakers (or whatever the chosen reference group is) and wish to use the language for certain functions, for example, regulating the behaviour of others, giving and receiving information, persuading and advising, recommending and denying, and so on. The word 'function' as used in linguistics and psycholinguistics has a variety of meanings. Here it is intended to refer to two interrelated kinds of information. The linguist Halliday (1970) distinguishes in general three kinds of global language function: the ideational, which is concerned with the organisation of ideas, the cognitive or propositional content of the message; the textual, which is concerned with the organisation and cohesion of language and its situational relevance; and the interpersonal, which is broadly concerned with the relationship between the form of language and the social setting it occurs in. The two senses of function to be discussed here are the textual and the interpersonal.

Psychologically one can view these categories of language behaviour as aspects of social skill. Argyle (1967) has argued that interpersonal behaviour, much of which is mediated via language, is analysable in terms of the learning of complex skills. Thus the development of their structure, timing, integration and responsiveness to feedback is analogous to that of the motor skills referred to in Chapter 3. According to this view, learning to choose language forms that are appropriate to what has gone before in the dialogue and to the situational context (the textual function), and learning to use the new language to interact with others in the way desired (and familiar in the first language) and to manage that interaction, open it, keep it going, take the desired turns to speak and close it when desired (the interpersonal function), are therefore teachable by methods derived from the learning of complex skills: by guidance, (guided discovery or modelling) by management of knowledge of results, by subdividing the task. Similar pedagogical problems also occur: selection and grading of communicative skills, part versus whole learning, massed versus distributed practice. However, since communicative skills are generally of a higher order of complexity, appropriate new methods also have to be developed.

In Chapter 4, discussing productive skills, the point was made that to make a meaningful utterance involves decisions at various levels, or of various kinds (about the discourse situation, the propositional content, the choice of words, the structure, and the phonology), but no illustrations for teaching were given. One approach which is common at low levels of proficiency is to remove the element of choice almost completely from the student, to support him in his attempts at situationally relevant and textually appropriate utterances by almost total control or guidance. For example, Ockenden (1972) has constructed substitution tables using whole sentences in short dialogues; once the student has learned the structure of a given dialogue, any of four versions of each turn of speaking will be an adequate precursor or answer to the surrounding ones. Ockenden's first dialogue, *Asking the way*, has the following turns:

(1) Attention-getting + request	*Excuse me, can you tell me where South Street is please?*
(2) Instruction with geography	*Take the second on the left and ask again.*
(3) Supplementary question (distance)	*Is it far?*
(4) Negative statement (reassurance)	*No, it's only about five minutes' walk.*
(5) Expression of thanks	*Many thanks.*
(6) Disclaimer	*Not at all.*

Other dialogues have different structures, believed to be more appropriate to the subject matter. For example, the response to a question or request is sometimes a question: dialogue 38 (*Asking favours*) has the following sequence:

(1) Request	*Is there any chance of borrowing your typewriter?*
(2) Question	*How long for?*

This type of substitution table aims at 'painless learning by heart' of the sentences in their appropriate contexts. It is claimed that boredom is avoided as, with a format of six turns and four possible realisations of each turn, there are 4096 possible different conversations. On the other hand, only a quarter of these differ by more than one sentence, and therefore the novelty is in fact considerably less dramatic than might be thought.

It may be argued that such absolute control over language and interaction pattern is useful at the earliest stages but is eventually counterproductive, as it does not provide for any material alteration or addition by the student. The difficulty is to arrange a smoothly graded sequence of relaxation of control into free conversational ability. One of the many problems here is how to develop exercises and activities that focus the student's ability to choose the linguistic form or packaging for what he wants to say (or for what the teacher wants him to say), which will be appropriate in the linguistic context and the situational context (again borrowing terms from Halliday). This problem ranges from the choice of structure to allow certain detailed elements of a message to be thematised, such as learning to use the passive voice to focus on the object or suppress the agent, by placing the agent at the end or omitting it, to the construction of longer messages, such as talks, and the written paragraph or essay. A simple oral focusing exercise is the following:

15.10   Watch closely as your teacher performs a number of separate actions. Answer his questions for each action.
1   (The teacher tears a sheet of paper into pieces)
   Teacher: *What happened?*
   Students: *You tore up a piece of paper.*
   Teacher: *What happened to the piece of paper?*
   Students: *It was torn up.*
2   (and so on)

(Rutherford, 1972, Vol. 1, p. 310)

With regard to the larger aspects of textual organisation, rather more work has been done in developing writing skills than speaking skills. Imhoof and Hudson (1975) display a relatively comprehensive approach to various forms of paragraph and essay organisation, based on the analysis of model paragraphs of several kinds and exercises for constructing them. Lawrence (1972) presents a graded sequence of exercises for training students to produce coherent and logical paragraphs.

In the field of conversational skills quite a lot of attention has recently been devoted to the use of role play for developing command of the interpersonal function in the new language. The concept of social role and role play and their use in education is by no means a new one; what is perhaps new is the use of this quasi-dramatic device with people who by definition do not have the linguistic skills to express the conventional expectations for that role, in order to develop just those skills. A role can be defined as 'the content common to the role expectations of the members of a social group' (Sarbin and Jones, 1956). This concept of role was first systematised in social psychology by Sarbin, who applied it to the concept of personality, claiming that personality was composed of several layers of interrelated role specifications and expectations of varying permanence and stability. A distinction can be drawn in role behaviour between role enactment, that is, performing a role that is part of one's normal life or personality, and role-playing, that is, pretending to react as if one were someone else in a different situation. Sarbin and Jones (1956) also showed that there existed a specific role-taking aptitude, such that however close people's stereotypes of certain roles might be, and however strong their motivation to take the roles, the validity of their role enactments or role plays might differ. Role-taking as a language teaching device should therefore be considered carefully with respect to the individual members of a particular class before it is adopted as a method. As social roles are intimately bound up with personality and the self, and as individuals differ in their role-taking aptitude, requiring some students to perform a role, whether familiar or new, in a foreign language, may possibly create tensions and worry which become counterproductive. Whether this can be avoided is partly a question of the degree and manner of linguistic support, that is, how much of the language necessary for the agreed role specification is known by or given to the student beforehand, and partly a question of the emotional climate of the classroom, primarily in terms of peer collaboration and trust. In general education, role-taking has been suggested as a technique for developing emotional reactions and understanding of others' opinions (see Good and Brophy, 1978). There is some evidence that role-taking is a powerful technique for manipulating opinion change (Janis and King, 1954). If this is the case, there is some sense in using it if the language syllabus also includes some cultural component.

One might divide the types of role-taking currently being developed in language teaching into: role enactment (playing oneself in a new situation); role-playing (pretending to be someone else); and role conflict (talking one's way out of a conflict of role expectations). There may be a good case to be made for using the three types graded in that order, on psychological grounds like those argued above, and on linguistic grounds as the language needed for the three probably increases in difficulty. An example of role enactment is the exercise used frequently in Jones's *Functions of English* (1977), in which language items and phrases are introduced and discussed and then used by the students:

2.8 *Presentation: getting further information*
You may often need to press people to tell you more than they have done in answer to a question. You may want further details or you may not be satisfied with the answer given. Here are some techniques for getting the extra information you want:
Could you tell me a bit more about that?
I'm not quite with you there.
Sorry, but could you explain that in a bit more detail, please?
I don't quite follow.
Sorry, that's not really what I mean, what I'd like to know is ...
Sorry to press you, but could you tell me ...
Sorry, I don't quite understand why.

Discuss with your teacher how these expressions would be used and what might be said before and after.

2.9　Practice

Ask your teacher to give you full details about what he does in the evenings and at weekends. Use the techniques presented in 2.8.

(Jones, 1977, p. 16)

The role here might be glossed as that of the 'incisive interviewer'; the language supports in the unit include polite questions, phrases for delaying and avoiding answering, and insistent probing.

A role-playing exercise might well be organised in the following way. A basic situation would be presented, with a set number of possible role relationships and as many turns at playing the roles as is feasible given the size of the group and the available time. Television interviewing might be a possible one for pairs of students. Other obvious ones would include doctor–patient pairs, shopkeeper–customer pairs, officialdom–client pairs; role plays for groups of three and five are also quite conceivable. General instructions are issued to the players including hints on the structure of the role play (for example, for interviewing, how to introduce the person, keep the flow of conversation going, close the interview), hints on the purpose of the role play (for example, eliciting, or keeping secret, the maximum information) and specific language items that the role-players will need. Specific role descriptions are provided for each participant which are usually not shown to anyone else. For the interviewing example, they might look like this:

Role Card　　Interviewer

You wish to interview Mr Smith because you think the nation should be able to decide whether his plan for a new type of insurance policy is a confidence trick or not. Be careful to be fair, but think of how to ask him when he had this idea, how it will operate, what his profits will be, what the customers will gain, what security he can offer, and what his background is.

Role Card　　Mr Smith

You have been in the world of finance for a relatively short time but believe you have discovered a way of bringing cheaper insurance to home- and car-owners. Some time ago you were well known as an actor but you left that profession. Think of the advantages of bringing cheaper insurance to people, how much money you can make at it, why people should trust you rather than other companies.

After the roles have been played and the planned number of students have acted this scene (with different personal details on the cards), the audience of non-participating students can be allowed to ask further questions, and the teacher can concentrate attention on language points arising, particularly if the role plays have been recorded.

One criticism of those kinds of role-taking exercise could be that they are disguised phrasebook learning, and it is notable that the language preparation tends to consist in the provision on cards, or by elicitation from the class, of key phrases which are to be incorporated. However, the purpose of a phrase book is to provide travellers with a list of unrelated but useful requests and inquiries that can be read out, when needed, outside the context of a normal conversation; the purpose of prepared role-taking is to give students the opportunity to practise constructing real conversations and using the new language to do some of the things they can already do in the first language. Watcyn-Jones (1978) has produced a whole textbook of role-play activities for a wide range of participant numbers. Some of the role plays in this textbook use pairwork for looking at data provided in the form of classified advertisements for houses, cars, jobs, and so on, from the different points of view of characters assigned on the role cards; individuals then report back the results to the whole group.

An example of a role conflict and resolution is afforded by Kettering's *Developing Communicative Competence* (1975). Here, individuals are asked how they would solve a social problem in English and talk their way out of a conflict situation. With Kettering's method possible solutions are volunteered and discussed, after preparation, by the student group; there need be no actual performance of the role.

Problem No. 3: Dinner at an American home
An American family asks you to dinner. They pick you up and take you to their home. They are very nice and try hard to make you forget how nervous and afraid you are about your English and the new customs. The wife has made a special dinner for you and has used her best dishes and tablecloth. She serves the food and you take a lot of the main dish to make her feel happy. You taste it and you *hate* it. It has liver in it and you never eat liver. She's waiting to see if you like the food. What do you do?
(Suggested solutions follow)

This section has discussed a few of the ways in which the classroom can become a dry run for the eventual goal of language teaching, the full functional use of language for communication. However, the classroom is itself a social setting, a very important one, and it is worthy of study in its own right.

The Classroom as a Social Setting

Emotional Climate

In the previous section, mention was made of the emotional climate of the classroom as a factor in the success of role-taking activities. This factor has, of course, far wider relevance than its application in those restricted circumstances. By 'emotional climate' is meant the complex nature of the learning atmosphere in the classroom, which is created by the teacher and the pupils and through which the teaching/learning operates. Its very complexity has made it a difficult concept to study. Early studies were concerned with establishing the relative success of certain identifiable teaching styles. Gage (1963) reviewed these and concluded that, despite the large variety of traits that had been investigated, such as warmth, indirectness, amount of talk, problem-solving ability, positive or negative control, authoritarian or democratic teaching styles and many others, the various studies were inconsistent with each other in definitions and in results and often 'lacking in psychological or educational meaning'. Nevertheless it is clear that the classroom groups do behave differently from each other and the same class may behave differently with different teachers; the methodological difficulties and lack of generalisability that have dogged so many of the researches in the area may best be regarded as only emphasising the intangibility of the classroom climate. Naturally, most of the interest and most of the applications of research into this question have been in general educational theory and in teacher training, but, apart from role play and other activities for training communicative skills, there are at least two quite important language teaching questions where classroom climate seems particularly important.

The first concerns the degree to which teachers can assume that students who are not actively participating in the classroom conversation are attending to it and learning from it. It was a tenet of audio-lingual theory that language, being a kind of behaviour, was learned only by performing that behaviour (see Chapter 2). This, at least as it was frequently interpreted, implied that language learning only takes place when the students are actively performing in the language. This belief was one of the motives behind the introduction of choral response techniques, to enable as many students as possible to learn by acting simultaneously, or co-acting, and behind the adoption of language laboratories, in which the whole class worked as individuals conversing with a taped partner. However, it would be wrong to assume that students do not learn when not overtly performing (either listening or responding in a conversation). As we saw in Chapter 2, a great deal of learning is incidental, that is, without obvious response or reward. Incidental learning in the classroom usually takes the form of learning by observation. However, whether or not a student will actually attend to the discussion between teacher and another student and learn from it, rather than merely watch for cues that the teacher might break off that conversation to ask someone else, depends on whether the climate of the class favours mutual dependence among the students or not. Some teaching authorities, for instance F. L. Billows (1961), have argued that one of the teacher's main functions is to design the kinds of activities that will encourage students to learn from each other and therefore be less dependent on the teacher.

The second instance, related to the first, is the question of group correction of errors. Students are often, understandably, unwilling to have their errors in written work exposed to their peers. One obvious reason for this is loss of face resulting from a punitive attitude to error. However, as we have seen in Chapter 3, errors are often evidence of improvement (though not obviously of perfection) and as such are an almost inevitable part of the learning process. Evaluation and correction of written errors by the group can be handled in several ways, including the overhead projector slide, so that each member can use his own and his peers' errors as information for building a more accurate conception of the various kinds of rules in the language that have been violated. This kind of collaboration is only possible if the teacher has fostered a non-hostile, trusting climate in the classroom.

The question of emotional climate is closely related to that of group cohesion. This term refers to the forces (apart from the timetable!) that bind a group together and give it a unity, a dynamic, which is different from the sum of the characteristics of the individuals which comprise it. As a general rule, group cohesion is increased by successful performance of group tasks, easy communication and eye contact between the members, competition with other groups, and lessened by repeated failure, disrupted channels of communication, competition within the group. Teachers in their role of managers of the learning group therefore exercise the options open to them of directly or indirectly influencing the group's dynamic by setting tasks at carefully chosen levels of difficulty, experimenting with seating arrangements, outside competitions and, in many cases, extramural activities. One very well-known note of caution has to be sounded, which is that group performance also decreases when cohesiveness is at a very high level; the enjoyment of being in the group outweighs the perceived advantages of completing the assigned, or chosen, task. This can manifest itself in several ways. One example is the falling-off of work-involvement and the quality of the group's productions. Another might be a group's excessive protectiveness towards one of its members in the kind of group error correction discussed earlier.

This kind of diminishing return was also found by Thelen (1967) in a rather different context, that of investigating the possibility of matching teachers' ideas of the kind of pupils they best succeeded with, with classes of pupils selected for their closeness to those characteristics. In his study the teachers then taught a matched class and a non-matched class for a year, and one can assume that in this time they managed, or did not manage, to build up the sort of cohesive and supportive atmosphere they preferred in their own classrooms. At the end of the year the matched classes were more work-oriented, less inattentive, less distractable, less rigid, more flexible, more permissive than the control classes, but the overall correlation with pupil achievement was zero – overall, the matched pupils did no better than the control pupils. Thus teachers should take care that their efforts to engineer the kind of classroom climate they are happiest to teach in, and they feel the students are happiest in, also further the expressed aims of the teaching.

Classroom language

The language used by teachers and pupils has been found by several authors working from different standpoints to have some interesting features. The functions of teacher and pupil talk are not always obvious to a casual observer, but exist meaningfully within a set of shared assumptions about the nature of the classroom game. Nash (1976) referred to this language as a kind of 'cryptic shorthand'. Bellack *et al.* (1966) showed that each lesson (in the native language; foreign language classes were not considered) had a kind of overall structure (not always the same as that planned by the teacher) which consisted of a series of pedagogical moves communicated by different kinds of language and non-verbal gestures. One move was 'structuring', when a participant, usually the teacher, said what procedure was to be followed; another was 'soliciting', when the teacher (usually) required some particular response, like an answer to a question; another was 'responding', usually the pupils' role; and lastly 'reacting', when teacher or pupils evaluated a response or expressed surprise, and so on. These were the basic moves in the game; one curious feature of the game is that for a teacher to win it, it is necessary for the pupils to be successful. Clearly foreign language lessons would make no exception to this kind of description, and frequently language teachers make a point of using certain phrases in the foreign language for each of the moves, from 'Open your books' (a structuring move which introduces a particular phase of activity like reading or answering questions) through 'Don't talk' (a reacting move) to 'Now you be the (policeman, customs officer, husband ...) and Jürgen the (criminal, traveller, wife ...)' (a structuring move) because they provide useful repetition even at a stage when the students do not know the full grammar of the phrases. There are several little published collections of such useful classroom phrases, and the main reason why they are useful is because the students are already very familiar with the moves and plays of the game they refer to. Sinclair and Coulthard (1975) used classroom language as the data for their linguistic analysis of discourse because of its relatively high degree of structure and predictability, and incorporated Bellack's notion of moves as one rank in their hierarchical description of discourse. Stubbs (1976) analysed teacher talk in rather different terms, as a shared code with nine specific functions, which, however, were rarely obvious from the actual language used, when considered out of context:

attracting or showing attention

controlling the amount of speech
checking or confirming understanding
summarising
defining
editing
correcting
specifying topic
maintaining topic.

This kind of research into classroom use of language has been pursued in general educational psychology for a variety of reasons, for example to draw out practical recommendations for trainee teachers, to decide between various teaching strategies from the point of view of their effectiveness, and to relate the kind of linguistic environment the school provides to the linguistic abilities of the members of the school in their mother tongue. However, the classroom use of a second or a foreign language is often the only regular exposure to the language the students have, and therefore the ways in which the language is typically used in the classroom are especially important. It was an assumption, for instance, in both the audio-lingual method and the cognitive-code (page 27) method that only grammatically correct utterances would be tolerated in the classroom, and that correction should follow immediately, sometimes with student repetition of the correct form, in cases of ungrammaticality. A further assumption was often made, that answers to questions should always be in the full form, thus repeating the contents of the question with a transformation:

> Q: *Is this a book on the table?*
> A: *Yes, this is a book on the table.*

Another widely held assumption was that teachers should exercise careful language control, only using words that have been explained and structures that have been drilled. A fourth was that structures must be learnt in isolation before dialogues and conversations can be engaged in. These assumptions, and others which together make up teachers' methods, have recently been challenged, sharpened or even invalidated by some of the descriptive work on second language learning in naturalistic and classroom contexts. It has frequently been noted that in first language acquisition the speech of young children is not always grammatically correct, although that of their parents probably is, and that the speech addressed to children is simplified in ways that parents and others (including older children) believe is understandable to the child. In untutored second language learning, according to Hatch (see Chapter 8), the learning of language structures arises out of involvement in real conversational interaction, and not the other way round. Whether or not further research confirms these ideas for other second language learning situations, the nature of classroom discourse in the foreign language is clearly important, and increasingly controversial.

Although classroom language is thus highly structured it does not necessarily follow any particular plan decided on by the teacher in the light of pedagogical convictions. This was shown by Mehan (1974), who analysed a lesson given by a foreign language teacher trainee and found that there were wide differences between what had happened, what was planned and what the teacher recalled of the lesson. Wragg (1970) also showed, using his own version of Flanders' system of interaction analysis adapted for foreign language classes, that the amount and kind of classroom business actually conducted in the foreign language was smaller than, and different from, what was recollected by the teacher. The techniques of interaction analysis have therefore been widely used for recording teacher behaviour and giving feedback to trainees, but the systems that have been developed are large in number, not based on any sound theory of classroom discourse, and take a long time to learn to operate satisfactorily.

One system, FOCUS, developed by Fanselow (1977) has received some attention in the context of foreign language learning. This system was developed in order to view teaching method and teacher effectiveness empirically, by seeing what kinds of communication took place in the classroom and what language functions were exercised. Thus language teaching method was to be researched at a level of specificity of classroom activity far more delicate than previously attempted in global discussions of the audio-lingual method or the cognitive-code method.

The major categories of the system are given below. Categories are grouped into five characteristics of communications, and each communicative exchange is described in terms of all five:

Who?	Purpose?	What medium?	How?	Content?
Teacher	structure	linguistic	attend	language
Student	solicit	non-linguistic	characterise	life
Group	respond	paralinguistic	present	procedure
Class	react		relate	subject matter
			re-present	

This type of analysis describes teaching acts in some detail, and each of the five characteristics of communications are indeed important but, unfortunately, there is no attempt to incorporate a functional linguistic analysis into the 'medium' characteristic. This is a serious defect, as the description otherwise demonstrates well the kinds of active student participation in the lesson which are allowed by the teacher's methodology. Perhaps the most important result secured by the use of systems of description such as FOCUS is the collection of hard data on the variety, or lack of it, of communicative acts in language classrooms. In fact, teachers rarely allow, or provoke, the full range of possibilities represented by such a grid. If the aim of language teaching is to produce students with communicative skill as well as grammatical knowledge, such a limited approach is counterproductive.

Another area of research on teacher talk has concentrated on the form of corrective feedback given by teachers (Allwright, 1975; Chaudron, 1977). Faced with a linguistic error by a student in oral work, a teacher must rapidly decide whether to ignore it, postpone correction until later, or deal with it immediately. If the third course is chosen, the teacher must further choose how to identify the error clearly (not an easy task) and how to treat it. To accomplish this, he or she can give the correct version, ask the transgressor to think again, or ask another student. Having treated it, the teacher decides whether to test the original transgressor in some way. After this whole exchange, the original topic has to be taken up again. At each stage the teacher's decision will be influenced by a number of considerations, such as the importance of the error, its frequency in the class, whether the correct version is in fact known to the student, possible loss of face by the student, or undesirable gloating by other students. All these decisions have to be taken fast in order not to interrupt the flow of the lesson. Teachers' preferred modes of treating error and the effectiveness of different modes of treatment are both being researched.

Small Group Instruction

Faced with the increasing need to produce students who command communicative skill as well as grammatical competence, and the realisation that classroom activities tend to be rather monotonous, many teachers and course writers have been looking for language teaching activities for small subgroups in the classroom. Many are also convinced that beyond the specific advantages for language teaching there are more general educational benefits, such as social learning and learning how to negotiate.

Many of the role-play exercises referred to above are designed for, or can be adapted for, small group work, with groups performing the roles worked out to the whole class at the end, for comparison or evaluation. Other techniques using group work revolve around the principle of task announcement or explanation, followed by small group collaboration on some aspect, followed by reporting back to plenary session. An example of this is the 'strip story' technique (Gibson, 1975, quoted by Rogers, 1978), in which a story is divided into one-line segments and printed on strips of paper. Each member of each group receives one strip, which he memorises and returns to the teacher; thus the members of each group have between them all the strips and therefore the whole story. All the groups' versions are then compared in plenary session. In assembling the story, the group needs information from every member, and argument will ensue about the correct order or expression of the various elements of the story. Rogers

(1978) has a valuable collection of group activities on this pattern and several other types. Lest it be thought, however, that communication skill training is only concerned with role play, games and imposed tasks such as this, it is important to emphasise that real communication consists in the effective use of language to express something that somebody wants to say. Thus even more important are 'buzz' group discussions (with the class divided into groups of three all 'buzzing' away in the foreign language for a short time) on real-life topics, perhaps provoked by some reading or listening passage. At a higher level, intensive group discussion of a student's presentation on a chosen topic (see, for instance, Kerr and McDonough, 1979) leads to real and often demanding communication practice. These are important because the students will be personally involved in the discussion, strategies such as turn-taking, and turn-maintaining will occur naturally and new vocabulary associated with the topic will be practised.

Cohesiveness

There are a number of factors affecting the success of small group work, apart from the inherent interest of its members in their task. We have already seen the slightly complex relationship between group cohesion and the quality of the group product. A reasonably high degree of cohesion is necessary before the members will change from co-acting as individuals working on their own to collaborating as a group with a collective responsibility to complete a task − whether this is a report to the whole class, or a questionnaire to be completed, or a problem to be solved. However, too high a degree of cohesion results in neglect of the group product in favour of enjoyment of being in the group (Davis, 1969, p. 75). In this situation, the teacher has the option either of changing the membership of the groups, or of setting very difficult tasks; both options lower cohesion.

Composition

The composition of the group is another important factor, and depends partly on the individual characteristics of the students. Some of the relevant individual differences are discussed in Chapter 9. At the beginning of group work, teachers ignore at their peril existing friendships and family relationships; but after a class is accustomed to group work those may no longer be important, as the cohesion of the group grows. For many tasks, groups can be given certain roles to elect among themselves, such as group leader and/or secretary; these can rotate. Rogers (1978) suggested that members also elect (or are elected to) other kinds of roles, such as 'smiler', 'moaner', 'opinion-giver', 'opinion asker'. This may help, by restricting the language the student has to use and by focusing his particular task; but it could also hinder, by restricting opportunity for real self-expression.

Size

Group size is another important variable, but teachers usually have to experiment to find the optimal size of group for their own classes. Optimal group size is usually a question of channels of communication (who can speak to whom and who can see whom) and this is severely constrained by seating arrangements. Language learning activities have been suggested for pair work, buzz groups of three or four and larger, role-taking groups. One organisational consideration is the possibility of reporting back to the whole class for general evaluation and comparison of the group's product. A class of forty working in pairs means twenty reports; groups of five would produce only eight reports, which would have a greater chance of reasonable discussion.

Co-operativeness

Group co-operativeness is a quality that has to be learned, since it is rarely obvious to students that the aim of the activity is a group product to which they all contribute. A number of techniques have been suggested for training groups for this, including brainstorming, in which ideas on some topic are solicited from all members in an uninhibited way, problem-solving sessions and simple games like 'getting it together' (Richardson, 1971, quoted in Rogers, 1978). Once this period of learning, if it is necessary, is over, the members of a co-operating group can discuss their tasks and reach decisions on them using language for an immediate communicative purpose in a way that is rarely provoked by traditional lockstep classroom organisation with the teacher drilling the whole class.

Arguments develop, information is shared, and gradually a complete picture is formed from individuals' contributions. Wight (1976) presented interesting evidence of this process in small group work with immigrant children:

Another example of children talking together involves Aleem and three (native speaker) friends (9 year olds). Aleem speaks Punjabi, Urdu and English. The four children have been given scissors and two 2" squares of paper which they have to bisect in different ways. They are working by themselves and are following instructions on a tape recorder. Terry and Fiona have bisected their squares on the diagonal, Aleem and Patsy have bisected theirs along the median.

Recorder:	*Do you notice what is happening to your shapes?*
Aleem:	*Yes, I been notice what happened, at first they go, first they go …*
Patsy:	*I noticed.*
Aleem:	*Listen!*
Terry:	*First they go in a square.*
Anon.:	*Sh sh*
Aleem:	*No, yeah they in a square the other one it goes in a oblong, then again it goes in a square.*

Fiona:	*Our one.*
Aleem:	*Then it goes in a oblong again.*
Terry and Fiona:	*Listen, listen, your one goes in a oblong and our one goes in a triangle. Then your one goes in a square and our one goes in a triangle again. Your one will go in a oblong and our one will go in –*
All:	*– a triangle.* (They have all spontaneously generated the two principles for the bisection of squares.)
Anon.:	*Yours actually gets –*
Aleem:	*Yours is only triangles, see it gets smaller and smaller*
Terry:	*You get squares, then a oblong.*

(Wight, 1976, pp. 4–5)

Co-operative groups are usually faster than individuals at solving problems. One of the reasons for this is that there are more sources of ideas and the memory load for steps in the solution is also shared. However, a successfully completed group task does not mean that every member of the group contributed equally, or even that every member understands the solution equally. This problem of unequal contributions is one of the most often quoted drawbacks of group work in language teaching. It requires great managerial skill on the part of the teacher to structure and control the groups so as to minimise the inequalities.

Productivity

One frequent argument for group work in language teaching is productivity, that is, the increased opportunity for meaningful and fairly realistic language use in simultaneous groups compared with the class acting as a whole, and the lower level of stress associated with speaking in a small group as against performing before a large class. Apart from the obvious problems of keeping the noise level down and preventing the use of the first language, the problem that teachers find most difficulty with here is that of error identification and correction. It is not feasible, or desirable, for the teacher to sit in as evaluator on all the groups, nor is it desirable for accuracy monitors to be appointed for each group. However, if each group has to decide on some group product, either in written or spoken form, in which to report the results of their session to the whole class, feedback can be given on errors made in that production, and errors made in the process of group deliberation left to themselves. As mentioned in the previous section, a teacher has always to weigh up the advantage of treating an error immediately against the disadvantage of disrupting the normal flow of conversation.

Social Distance

So far, in this chapter, we have looked at communication skill as an aim of language teaching and at some linguistic aspects of the classroom as a social unit. But success in learning foreign languages is often dependent on social factors outside the classroom. These concern the perceived status the foreign language has for the learning group and are communicated by pressure of public opinion and parental attitude. Schumann (1976) coined the term 'social distance' for these factors, and argued that language learning situations could be evaluated from good to bad according to a complex of eight different dimensions which together define the distance between two groups or language communities in terms of social solidarity and affect individuals' learning as members of one of the groups. Schumann's eight dimensions are as follows, and their effect is the net result of the difference between the language learning group's view of the target language group and of the target language group's view of the learners:

(1) Dominance: political, cultural, technical, economic.
(2) Characteristic integration pattern: which ranges from adoption of the lifestyle of the target language group by the learning group to rejection of that lifestyle.
(3) Enclosure: the degree of separation and independence of institutions such as schools, churches, professions, and so on.
(4) Cohesiveness of the group.
(5) Size, particularly of the learning group.
(6) Congruence of the two cultures.
(7) Attitudes.
(8) Intended length of residence.

Good language learning situations occur where the target language group agrees with the learning group in being non-dominant, desiring an adaptive integration pattern and having low enclosure, and where the learning group has low cohesion, small size, a congruent culture, positive attitudes and intends to stay a long time. Variations from this pattern comprise a gradient of evaluation. Schumann reports one case of a Spanish-speaking immigrant to the United States, a labourer, who appears to have failed to learn English because of a set of perceptions of social distance between English-speaking Americans and Spanish-speaking Mexicans which created the worst pattern for language learning. In this pattern his group of Latin American workers and English-speaking Americans agreed that the learning group was subordinate, wanted to preserve its own identity and therefore had a rejecting integration pattern, and wanted moderate enclosure, and that the learning group had high cohesion and was large. Attitudes and intended length of residence do not seem to have been elicited in this case.

The concept of social distance, which was conceived after consideration of the social situations in which pidgin languages develop, is a useful beginning for unravelling the complex burden of social roles, preconceptions and hindrances that a learner brings to the language learning situation by virtue of being a member of a group whose language is in contact with another group's. In some cases the teacher's job is complicated by the hope that some of the barriers to learning can be broken down; in others, persistent failure may be explained by social factors rather than specific learning disabilities, or even ineffective teaching. However, these social factors have to be seen also in the light of other influences on students' motivation, which we shall look at in more detail in Chapter 10.

Summary

In this chapter we have reviewed implications for language teaching of the social nature of language, with regard to the textual and interpersonal aspects of communication skill; the social psychology of some communicative activities such as role-taking; the social psychology of the classroom and of classroom language; and social-psychological aspects of group work. Finally a brief comment was made on wider sociological issues affecting language learning via the social distance across which members of learning groups and members of groups speaking the desired language view each other.

Chapter 7

First Language Acquisition

It is manifestly impossible to condense into one short chapter the great amount of research into child language that has been reported in the last fifteen to twenty years. Nevertheless, some of the issues that that research has raised have important implications for the study of second or foreign language acquisition. Therefore there follows a selection of those issues which appear at the moment to the writer to be the ones of greatest relevance to those concerned with the study of the acquisition of additional languages.

As pointed out in Chapter 1, no material distinction between the terms 'learning' and 'acquiring' is intended. Since one of the central questions to which research has been devoted is whether or not the process of becoming articulate in the second language is the same as in the first, and since this question has not yet been satisfactorily resolved, the two terms will be used interchangeably here. Other texts have tried to draw distinctions between them, but none so far proposed is satisfactory.

It is usually assumed that children and adolescents or adults are quite different types of learner, for example, because of the spontaneous nature of language acquisition by children and the contrasting, more cerebral, logical processes of the adult. For this reason one might well ask: why look at child language acquisition at all? The answer to this is fourfold:

(1) Children are the best examples of language learners we have; it would seem sensible to study how they perform the task to see if any features can be generalised to language learning at later stages, or if there are good reasons to believe that such generalisations are impossible.

(2) Several second language teaching methods have embodied the claim that learning a second language recapitulates learning the first language. To evaluate this claim, we must have good descriptions of both processes; otherwise, comparisons between first and second language learning will remain at the level of mystery and doctrine.

(3) It has often been argued that learning a second language reactivates the

processes by which the first language was learnt, and that therefore the learning will be that much more efficient the closer together the two experiences are in time. This has been used as an argument supporting the introduction of a foreign language in the primary school; a study of the processes that are, allegedly, reactivated is necessary before this argument can be evaluated.

(4) Child language acquisition may be a unique phenomenon. It has been claimed that neither the behaviourist nor the cognitive information-processing approaches to learning can explain certain crucial facts about child language, for example, the creation of novel utterances, the universality of the order and rate of learning, and the child's discovery of rules that apparently operate at a level deeper than the sounds he or she hears, the so-called structure-dependent nature of the rules. (As an illustration of this last point, consider what has to be learned in order to put the correct phrase after *by* in these examples:

> *The man always makes breakfast⟶*   *Breakfast is always made by the man*
> *The man in the pink pyjamas makes breakfast⟶*
> *Breakfast is in the pink pyjamas made by the man.*

The rule shifting the psychological subject to the end must operate at an abstract level of structure to avoid the error in the last sentence.) Since all second language learners have already gone through this experience, the second language teacher needs a description of the phenomenon to understand where the learner's starting point is, and how learning a new language may differ from learning other subjects.

Rules or Habits?

Behaviourist theories applied to child language acquisition have strongly emphasised the role of the environment in providing both stimuli for imitation and also reinforcement, either positive or negative, for responses. According to these theories, only the external environment offers both the model of the language and the mechanism whereby responses are (a) selected for correctness, (b) discriminated for appropriateness to a stimulus and (c) generalised to new situations. Such a system can be attacked on many grounds, but the two most important for our purposes are theoretical and empirical.

Noam Chomsky, in his famous review of Skinner's *Verbal Behaviour* (1959), pointed out that these concepts of stimulus, response, reinforcement, generalisation, and so one, could not be given any satisfactory definitions when removed from the narrow world of animal experimentation in puzzle boxes and 'Skinner boxes'. As we have seen in Chapter 2, in a typical Skinnerian behaviour shaping experiment an animal is trained to perform some action by being put through a schedule of reinforcement which, by alternately rewarding and withholding reward, selects some observable aspect of the animal's behaviour, increases its probability of occurrence, links it with some other action, and so builds up a complex chain of behaviour which the animal performs if rewarded. The behaviour is observed, the reinforcement is physical. In the case of complex human behaviour like language, it is much less easy to say what has been observed. If a child says *Mama*, is that a simple set of sounds, or does it express some relationship such as a request – *I want Mama* – or a directive such as *Mama get me a toffee*? Since reinforcers are supposed to follow observable responses, there should be a more satisfactory definition of response. The concept of reinforcer is equally difficult to define, at least outside the experimental situation. A reinforcer is defined in terms of the increased strength of the response it followed – in other words, if it reinforced, then it was a reinforcer. Chomsky argued that when applied in areas of complex human activity outside the experimental training session these terms were either trivial in the amount they could explain or vacuous – devoid of meaning.

Nevertheless, the basic idea that language learning is a matter of imitation, generalisation and analogy is an empirical proposal which also requires an empirical refutation. There have been several reports of facts about child language which challenge this (Berko, 1958; Ervin, 1964), but the most dramatic is the phenomenon of regularisation. When a child begins to use past tense meanings, he uses some of the small set of common, irregular forms such as *went*, *broke*, *slept*, *ate*, presumably following the models in his speech environment. They do not always correspond, however, to the adult meanings, indicating that, for example, for the child, *went* is not part of the same verb as *go*. There follows a stage where all past tense forms are regularised, that is, they are all formed as if a rule 'present tense form + *-ed*' had been learnt, and this is applied indiscriminately even to those verbs which had previously had the correct form. Later on – after a matter of years – the irregular forms emerge again. The stage of regularisation is evidence for the creation of a rule precisely because, in the first place, those forms which were correct and could have been imitated are replaced by forms which have never been heard by the child and, secondly, forms which, according to a reinforcement theory, must have been reinforced are replaced by forms generalised by analogy which, however, have not been reinforced.

It is now widely believed that a proportion of a child's language acquisition time is spent in creating for himself a rule system which enables him not only to make errors such as overregularisation, but also to construct novel sentences which he has heard no one produce and which are nevertheless consistent with the rest of his language.

Constraints on Rule Creation

To say that each child puzzles the grammatical system out for himself unaided does not mean to say that no guidance, or constraints on his rule invention, is or are available to the child either from within himself or from aspects of his environment. It has been argued that a process of rule creation alone could not ensure:

(1)   the universality of language acquisition, both in the sense that all humans in all cultures appear to learn language in broadly similar ways (though the evidence for this is actually scanty), and in the sense that even severely mentally retarded children learn some recognisable language skills such as naming (Lenneberg, 1964);

(2)   the detailed knowledge of a language that every native speaker has;

(3)   the apparent speed of language acquisition (though we shall see later that there are some syntactic constructions which are not correctly used until the child is nearly 10);

(4)   the apparent independence from an instructor.

Arguments have been raised for and against each of these points but, briefly, the trend has been to suggest that the child's rule construction process is informed by, and perhaps constrained by, one or more of the following sources: innate preconceptions about language structure, processes in the child's linguistic and non-linguistic interaction with other children and adults, and non-verbal things learnt in the pre-speech period, such as the usual structure of action in the real world.

The strongest claim concerning genetic transmission of language is represented by the suggestions of Chomsky (1965), McNeill (1966), and others, that some general information about language structure is programmed in the genetic code and therefore available to the child before he begins to puzzle out the structure of the speech he hears around him. This could be glossed as a 'content' approach. Its proponents have argued that the child must know certain facts which are true of all possible human languages (though not, of course, features specific to any particular language), against which he can check his hypotheses about the structure of the language in his environment, so that he only progresses further with hypotheses that do not conflict with universal features of human language. These features are thought to be of two sorts: formal universals, such as the idea that all languages exhibit two levels of structure, underlying and superficial, which are interrelated in complex ways, and substantive universals, such as a limited set of possible distinctive features for the sounds of speech (which is not surprising, since all humans have the same speech organs). There must also be, according to this proposal, a criterion for preferring one hypothesis over another. In short, this proposal encompasses a language acquisition device specifically for language which is part of the child's inherited human character, consisting of (a) substantive universals, (b) formal universals, (c) evaluation procedure. Several predictions follow from this kind of content theory, but here we will pursue only one of them: the prediction that, since the child already 'knows' that there are two levels of analysis, he will invent hypotheses consonant with that. The development of the passive form in English is a good example. (It is acquired relatively late, but that is not important in this connection.) Chomsky's proposal predicts that, since the child is primed with the knowledge of two levels of structure, syntactic forms that are close to the underlying structure will be easier for him than syntactic forms that are not. In Chomsky's own transformational description of the English passive, the underlying form is that with an agent-phrase:

A *The stone was thrown by John*

and the so-called short form is produced by deletion of the agent-phrase:

B *The stone was thrown*

Chomsky's acquisition device therefore predicts that children will learn these two forms in the order A, B because A is 'simpler' than B. In fact, children produce B-type sentences much earlier than A-type ones. For children, B-type sentences appear to be a development of simple noun-verb-adjective sequences:

The stone was grey
The stone was thrown

and the full passive appears to derive from these by addition of an agent (Derwing, 1973; Aitchison, 1976). Of course, one counter-example does not demolish a theory, but similar arguments can be made about the development of adverbial clauses, relative clauses and other complex structures (Aitchison, 1976). This result from child language acquisition puts the discussion of psycholinguistic assumptions at the beginning of Chapter 4 in a different light. There is an important difference, of course, in that the discussion in Chapter 4 was about selection and sequencing of presentation, whereas here we are concerned with a pattern of errors of production. Nevertheless, the parallel between Method A and the sequence of development here is striking.

Another kind of approach to language acquisition has been called a 'process' theory. A process theory makes a much weaker claim about the nature of the innate endowment for language, namely, that while some specifically linguisitic information is transmitted genetically, the process of acquisition of a child's first language is also dependent on several other factors; these include the cognitive processes that are part of the child's general cognitive equipment by which he learns, for example, to make sense of visual sensations and perceive visual forms. The suggestion is that the child enters the world with several built-in basic perceptual strategies which enable him to begin understanding any language with a reasonable chance of success, before experience of interaction in the language can develop the complexity and subtlety of the adult's intuitions about the language. Research into visual perception has shown (Bever, 1970) that children have a notion of more/less than five objects at a very early age; this is an example of a basic perceptual strategy, and one that eventually develops into a simple form of generative grammar, the number system. (It is generative in that even the least numerate of us can understand, and occasionally produce, numbers that we have never before seen or heard — even the notion of infinity — by applying a simple and finite set of rules.) Slobin suggests that a child is equipped, probably innately, with a set of 'language definitional universals', which embody in a very general way the basic similarities between all languages.

> Everywhere language consists of utterances performing a universal set of communicative functions (such as asserting, denying, requesting, ordering, and so forth), expressing a universal set of underlying semantic relations, and using a universal set of formal means (such as combinable units of meaning made up of combinable units of sound, etc). (Slobin, 1973, p. 179)

However, the process of language acquisition, in particular the order in which expressive devices are acquired, is governed, according to Slobin, by a set of operating principles or self-instructions which the child maintains. They are heuristic, that is, more like informed guesses, and are used to help the child perceive the structure and meaning of the language he hears. These principles help him to discover meaning in what he hears and, from the language definitional universals and from the processing limitations imposed by his small capacity of storage and computation, to derive general cognitive-perceptual strategies.

Slobin argues that constraints on the order of acquisition of structural devices are best seen in cases of simultaneous acquisition of two languages, and in cross-language comparisons. He gives the example of children who are growing up to be bilingual in Hungarian and Serbo-Croat in a region of northern Yugoslavia. Locative expressions in Hungarian are indicated by an unambiguous noun suffix, for example:

hajó-ban = in the boat

whereas in Serbo-Croat they are indicated by a preposition that takes a case ending, and the meaning of the preposition changes with different case endings, for example:

u kuću = in the boat

Children growing up speaking these two languages in fact learn the correct Hungarian forms for expressing location first.

On the basis of a study of two of these children he argues that the explanation for the Hungarian forms being learnt first is the perceptual salience of the ending, the suffix. In other words, children tend to notice, and learn first, forms which vary regularly in their endings. The operating principle he suggests, as a summary of a large amount of data on this point, is very simple: A Pay attention to the ends of words. It is modified by another principle: B The phonological forms of words can be systematically modified. On the basis of similar bilingual and cross-language data, Slobin makes a number of other suggestions for operating principles:

(C) Pay attention to the order of words and morphemes.
(D) Avoid interruption or rearrangement of linguistic units.
(E) Underlying semantic relations should be marked overtly and clearly.
(F) Avoid exceptions.
(G) The use of grammatical markers should make semantic sense.

It will be noticed that these concern both the form of utterances and also the relation between the semantic intention and the forms.

Whether one accepts a strong claim for a universal, innate, language-specific component, or a weak one using some innate language knowledge and some factors from general cognitive equipment and learned skills, it is still reasonable to ask if the constraints which govern the acquisition of the mother tongue also affect the learning of additional languages. In fact, evidence that might bear on this question is scanty.

Similarities between first and second language learning, which will be discussed in the next chapter, may simply be due to contributions from one experience to the next and not by themselves constitute evidence for an innate component in second language learning. The innate component in first language acquisition has been linked to the development of cerebral dominance and the increased specialisation of brain areas involved in language (Lenneberg, 1967); a critical period for language acquisition might end when this process is complete. The age at which this is thought to take place might be not more than 5 years (Krashen, 1973). If, however, the main mechanisms of language learning are based on general cognitive operating principles, there is no reason to suppose a critical period should exist at all. There is evidence that older children and adults are in fact better at learning second languages than younger children (Fathman, 1975; Ervin-Tripp, 1974); the belief that primary schoolchildren were *ipso facto* better language learners than older children, used as one of the arguments for the inclusion of foreign languages in the primary school curriculum, has not been upheld.

Other Sources of Information

There have been several attempts to explain language development in terms of the experience the child gains before he is capable of uttering his first word. For example, two major classes of linguistic function, asserting (that is, making statements about the presence of some object) and requesting (that is, asking for attention and/or asking for some object), are present in the pre-speech period in non-verbal form. A child will often point to an object to indicate either its presence or his recognition of it, and he will reach for or grasp the conversation partner in soliciting attention or demand some object by reaching for it. While it is tempting to see a continuity between these non-verbal actions and the later development of linguistic grammar, there is an evident gulf to be bridged by developmental theory. One researcher who has attempted to show how linguistic form develops as a result of the communicative functions the child acquires is Halliday (1975, for example). In an extensive study of his own son he has outlined how the child began with a very limited set of functions, each of which was signalled unambiguously either by a word or an intonation pattern, and then he elaborated them. As the number of words the child could produce increased so the language used for each of these functions became more complex and interdependent, until the child achieved the adult recognition that the form of language and its functions were not in a one-to-one correspondence, and that the same syntactic and phonological forms might express more than one function depending on situation, knowledge about the listener and intonation pattern.

Another approach to language acquisition in the general area of communicative function is Bruner's (1975) suggestion that linguistic structure, in particular the devices in language for presenting topics and comments, or 'theme' and 'rheme', develops out of the child's pre-existing conception of the structure of co-operative action. In other words, a child learns to communicate using very basic distinctions of topic and comment, subject and predicate, agent, action and goal by virtue of having perceived and experienced interactions, usually with the mother, in which action, gesture and holophrases are combined to regulate his or someone else's attention, or interactions in which the child solicits the mother's attention and the mother responds to the action by playing some game like 'Peek-a-boo'. Bruner makes the strong claim that: 'the child comes to recognise the grammatical rules for forming and comprehending sentences by virtue of their correspondence to the conceptual framework that is constructed for the regulation of joint action and joint attention' (1975, p. 18).

Other investigators have concentrated on the language and behaviour of those in the child's environment. Although earlier in this chapter we rejected the idea of environmental control in the sense of reinforcement, and attempts to demonstrate linguistic reinforcement have usually failed, it is nevertheless possible that the type of model of the language provided and the pattern of interaction given should be regarded as crucial to the child's linguistic development. To judge by the way adults talk to children, they seem to have the impression that certain types of utterance will not be understood by the child, and they adapt their language accordingly. This adapted language has received the name 'Motherese'. Motherese is characterised by two sorts of adaptations: simplification strategies and clarification strategies (Ferguson, 1964). Mothers and other people use simpler structures in speaking to their children than they do among themselves; and they clarify the interaction by using many devices for securing the child's attention (exaggerated intonation, frequent naming, and so on) and repeating either something they said in many different sentence frames (*Pick up the red one. I want the red one. No, the red one.*) or what the child said, as if to check whether they have heard it correctly. It has been suggested that three general types of language lessons are being made available to the child here:

(a) Lessons about how to conduct conversations, take turns, initiate topics, make requests, and so on. These lessons come in the form of attention getters, directives and prompts (*now you*).

(b) Lessons about the meanings of words. These come from supplying words when the child's need is clear, and from giving contextual clues to new words.

(c) Lessons about where words, and other constituents, begin and end. These come from pauses, repetitions, and familiar frames for new words: e.g. *There's an oak tree.*
(Clark and Clark, 1977, p. 329)

Certain lessons do not seem to be viable: syntactic correction, for example, usually makes no difference to the child's behaviour, and neither does correction of pronunciation. That is to say, the child's syntax and pronunciation will approximate those of his environment regardless of overt correction by the parent. There are still unanswered questions about the lessons that do appear to take place: whether they have any effect, that is, whether the child actually learns from them, and whether they are a necessary condition of development, for example.

Syntactic Development

A large literature on syntactic development exists, inspired generally by transformational views on syntax. We have, however, already seen that a transformational analysis of the adult target structure is not an adequate basis for a theory of acquisition, and that children appear to use heuristic operating principles in making sense of these structures and consequently make errors in comprehension and production. To illustrate the quite large time-period which is required for mastery of syntactic structure, we will look at some examples: the appearance of various functors, question forms, the *easy/eager* distinction, and verb complements.

R. Brown (1973) and his colleagues showed early in their research that children go through a stage when their production is limited to a certain number of meaningful forms, and that this steadily increases. At the two-word stage the two words that are produced (either spontaneously or as imitations) sound like a reduced, telegraphese form of an adult utterance:

Daddy car

There have been several suggestions as to how to write grammars to capture the child's linguistic knowledge at this point, but no generally acceptable solutions. Telegraphese is typically full of stresses, content words; the little words and inflections (prepositions, *'s, to, 'd, 'll,* etc. that adults use to express grammatical functions are absent. These are added in what might be a consistent, natural order; which means that there is a recognisable consistency among native learners of English as to which function words they can use correctly when they want to express the appropriate meaning. For example, the *-ing* form appears very early, correctly meaning an ongoing process; the preposition *in* follows, *on* comes next, and *-s* is added first to nouns to make plurals, then to nouns to make possessives, but much later to pronouns or nouns to make a copula (*He's a spaniel*) and later still to the same forms to make an auxiliary (*He's sitting*). This may be seen as part of the child's realisation that the expectation expressed as strategy B by Slobin is not particularly useful for English – phonologically identical suffixes mean different things on different words.

Question forms appear to go through several steps: first of all, a *wh*-question word (usually *what* or *where*) is simply attached at the beginning of a little sentence; next, different question words (*why*) are added, not always, however, with a new meaning (that is, *why* sometimes equals *where*); then, after the child has acquired auxiliary verbs, the verb and subject can be inverted. Typically, the inversion appears correctly in *yes/no* questions earlier than it does in *wh-* questions. By and large, this is a picture of the child painfully learning to put new syntactic operations together, and it takes a long time. One should notice that only part of the difficulties are syntactic: the use of an auxiliary, which is used elsewhere correctly first. The consistent appearance of *why* and its inconsistent meaning is perhaps due to a cognitive process. It would be reasonable to suggest that questions of identity and place (*what* and *where*) precede questions of causality and perhaps time (*why* and *when*) because of their relative conceptual difficulty, but one cannot use that as an explanation without some independent measure of cognitive development.

It has often been suggested that a child has acquired the basic grammatical structure of the language by the age of 5. However, children have to reach a mental age of over 6 years before they can consistently understand adjectives such as *easy* and *eager* correctly in constructions such as

The wolf is eager to bite

The duck is easy to bite
(Cromer, 1970)

Most children begin by interpreting such sentences as if the surface subject (the duck and the wolf) was doing the action of the infinitive verb; then there follows a period of inconsistency, and after about a mental age of 6 years 8 months the two structures are handled separately, and correctly. This suggests that such differences of underlying structure are difficult for the child to recognise until he has a certain level of intellectual functioning: in other words, this is an aspect of language (and a very general principle, used by Chomsky to indicate the necessity for a deep level of analysis) which the child does not seem to be innately programmed to search for.

An element of structure which is acquired even later is linguistically related to this: the grammar of complement constructions. C. S. Chomsky (1969) pointed out that children fail to understand sentences in which the subject of the verb in the complement phrase is not the nearest noun phrase, until they are relatively old. The ages at which this is understood are not fully determined (see Kessel, 1970), but it appears to be between 7 and 9, later than the *easy/eager* distinction. In question are sentences like:

(1) *John tells Jim to speak*
(2) *John asks Jim to speak*
(3) *John asks Jim what to do*
(4) *John promises Jim to speak.*

In (1) and (2) Jim will *speak*, whereas in (3) and (4) John will *do* and John will *speak*. The complement pattern following verbs like *tell* is acquired earliest; the patterns following *ask* are acquired later, after passing through a period of inconsistency, and the pattern of *promise* comes last. Perhaps the reason for this is to be found in the violation of strategy D: Avoid interruption of linguistic units.

Syntactic development was the first aspect of second language learning to be investigated systematically, and therefore it has received the greatest amount of attention (see Chapter 8). However, it is obvious that second language learners know (by virtue of speaking a language already, although they may not have conscious awareness or the power to formulate their knowledge) a great deal about syntactic structure: for example, that it is hierarchical, that its surface forms are often ambiguous and that its relation to language functions is multifarious. It is by no means obvious that first language learners have this kind of knowledge when they begin. This is perhaps a crucial difference between the two language learning situations.

Word-Meaning

Children learn words and their meanings in several different ways. It is a frequent observation that they very often use one word for many apparently unconnected objects. For example, *bow-wow* might be used to refer to a dog, an uncle, and a train. Vygotsky (1962) referred to this as a 'heap' kind of concept. Presumably there is some connection apparent to the child; it is not always easy to see what it might be. The frequent phenomenon of overextension has received several explanations. Sometimes a label may be attached to all objects that seem to the child to have some element in common (for example, all things that have feature X); or, it may be attached to a collection of objects which have some, but different, things linking them (for example, a *bow-wow* may be a dog, an uncle who has a dog, and a train because the uncle gave the boy a train). The development of labelling is thus intricately bound up with the child's intellectual development and his concept-formation ability. Another important point here is that children are by no means uniform in their vocabulary development; Nelson (1973) has shown several dimensions of individual differences.

One aspect of intellectual functioning which seems to be necessary for the acquisition of language forms is the gradual abandonment of egocentricity, the child's tendency to take only his own perspective into account. Young children typically make mistakes in giving or receiving directions, not realising that left and right are reversed for a person who is sitting facing them. A more subtle instance is the use of the definite article. In English it is presupposed that the object denoted by the noun after the word *the* has been identified by both speaker and hearer, or by speaker for hearer. Adults behave in exactly this way (Osgood, 1971). A child at a certain stage, however, is able to use *the* for something specific to him, but fails to realise it is not identified for the hearer. Thus, one of R. Brown's (1973) children (Sarah) said, *I want to open the door* and her mother replied, *What door?* Sarah presumably believed that since it was obvious to her which door was meant, it was obvious to all. She had no conception of an addressee having a different state of knowledge.

In other areas of vocabulary it has been suggested (E. Clark, 1973) that children build up the meanings of words and thus the correct adult use of these words by adding one semantic feature at a time. By feature, in this context, is meant a component of meaning that is shared by a number of different words. Thus, the dimensional term *big* shares a component of meaning with each of the other words which only refer to single dimensions: it shares 'height' with *tall*, 'horizontally' with *wide*, 'going away from speaker' with *deep*, (as in *a big cupboard*), 'extension' with *long*, and like all those unidimensional terms it is implicitly gradable – that is, we say 'it's big' compared to the normal size for that kind of object. Children tend to begin by using *big* and *little* as global antonyms. Other dimensional terms they use (*long*, *wide*, and so on) are initially incorrectly interpreted as each other and as *big* and *little* (Eilers *et al.*, 1974). Only later are individual dimensions perceived and separated off, and then the individual specific dimensional terms are used more correctly. Oddly enough, this trend is accompanied by a period in which *big* is no longer used correctly.

Other adjective pairs show an analogous trend. For example, children tend at first to respond to *more* and *less* as if they were synonymous, meaning 'a quantity of', or 'some'. At a later stage, both terms are used with the meaning 'a greater quantity of', or 'more'. Later still, they are distinguished, with the isolation of the negative feature in *less* (= 'not more') (Donaldson and Balfour, 1968).

However, this feature-by-feature type of theory does not seem to be true of adjectives like those of colour. Colour terms appear to be attached first to focal colours. That is, when the term *red* is first used consistently, it is used by the child to denote that shade of red regarded by adults as the best example of pure redness, that is, the focal red, and it is also learnt before terms that do not refer to focal colours in this sense, like *puce* and *beige* (Heider, 1971). It might well be that this focal red is predetermined by the physiological properties of the visual system, and cross-cultural research on basic colour terms (Berlin and Kay, 1969) has shown that there is a wide measure of agreement between language communities and cultures as to the hues that are focal. Quite a lot of research is now being conducted to see what other areas of vocabulary might be the result of this sort of biological predisposition (Rosch, née Heider, 1973).

It should be obvious from this short exposition that there are several theories and it may be that different areas of vocabulary and kinds of semantic classifications are acquired in different ways. The second language learner develops the vocabulary of the new language primarily by attaching new words into an already formed conceptual system. Although naturally there are many cases, perhaps the majority, where the words of the new language blur and re-draw distinctions of meaning, the second language learner already has a coherent set of concepts and semantic features and does not have to build a new one at the same time as he/she acquires the language. Thus with the second language one can speak of acquiring vocabulary, and the meanings current within that speech community; with the first language it is difficult to separate cognitive development from linguistic development.

Conclusion

In the next chapter we will consider some of the evidence that second language acquisition is similar to the pattern sketched here for first language acquisition. If the processes are similar, one would expect (a) similar patterns of error from adults learning English, from children learning English as an additional language and from native children acquiring English, and (b) similar orders of acquisition in the three cases: adults, child bilinguals and monolingual children. However, the degree of similarity to be expected should not be overstated. In the case of the first language, we have seen that the notion of an operating principle or strategy has been a useful construct. The L_2 learner may also use a set of such operating principles in working out the structure of the new language. The details of the expectations may, however, be rather different and two suggestions at least have been put forward to account for the difference. First, the expectations will have been affected by the native language, because he/she will have refined the original operating principles, perhaps discarded some, in the process of acquiring it. Secondly, he/she may have forgotten how he learnt his first language (if he/she was ever aware of learning it in the first place) and come to the new task with quite unrelated assumptions.

As well as considering rather abstract notions of learning strategies and cognitive development, we have considered the social setting of language development and looked at the possibility that adults give children unconscious language lessons. One should not take the word 'lesson' too seriously, redolent as it is of carefully constructed pedagogy, but there may be important clues there as to how the learner of an additional language may be benefiting from classroom talk. Clearly children learn many sociolinguistic, semantic and structural elements incidentally, from the sociolinguistic mechanisms of their conversations with their peers and adults. This kind of unplanned, probably unconscious, learning from the organisation of interaction may also take place in the second language classroom. Krashen (1977) has argued that older children and adult second language learners may both acquire language as they did their first languages, and learn the rules in the ways usually required in formal teaching. Krashen thereby assumes that the ability to benefit incidentally from the available information about the new language without conscious attention remains with the individual from childhood, although he recognises there are wide differences in individual approaches to second language learning. Independent evidence of the existence of these two processes, which he considers as complementary in his monitor model, is needed, and this possible basis for a distinction between learning and acquisition will be taken up again in the next chapter.

Perhaps the most important benefit to the foreign language teacher from a concern with first language acquisition is the recognition that errors may be systematic and indicative of active organisation of the language data by the learner. Not only may the path to the adult grammar lie through thickets of errors, but in the early stages there may well be deceptively 'correct' behaviour. As we have seen, increasing frequency of errors (for example in past simple tense forms) may indicate the shift away from a simple conception of the rule system, which happens to match the demands made on the child's language at the time, towards a more complex but more generally valid rule. Paradoxically, therefore, getting worse temporarily may be evidence for getting nearer the target grammar. We shall see in the next chapter if this also occurs in second language learning.

Chapter 8

Second Language Learning

Since the publication of S. P. Corder's article 'The significance of learners' errors' in 1967 it has become increasingly widely recognised that the course of learning a language by a non-native speaker is a fascinating and fruitful field of research. Research has, in the past, been devoted to comparisons of methods of instruction; to comparisons between the mother tongue and the target language; to ways of extrapolating insights from general psychology to language learning and incorporating them as features of instruction; and to the differences between individual learners which exist before the learning experience and can interact with learning performance, like aptitude, attitudes and motivation. It is only comparatively recently, no doubt encouraged by the great advances made in the methodology of language acquisition research by those studying child language, that researchers have begun to find ways of elucidating and demonstrating systematic features of the process of acquisition of second language.

Despite the effort that has been put into various kinds of research into second language learning recently, the impact of the theories and results thus generated on language teaching methodology has as yet been limited. Notwithstanding, this kind of research holds considerable promise of useful information for the language teaching profession. First, teachers' attributions of the causes of student error can be sharpened and given weight. For example, persistent errors may be due to some inherent difficulty in the new language, transfer from the mother tongue, limited exposure to a good and consistent model of the new forms, lack of penalty in the form of communication failure, or laziness. Research on other learners can aid a teacher in attributing a cause to an error produced by the learner and therefore in giving corrective feedback or other treatment. Secondly, syllabuses can be planned and sequenced in the light of hard evidence from real learners, not just extrapolations from descriptions of languages and learning from general linguistics and general psychology. So far, most of the literature on second language learning has concentrated on the development of syntax and vocabulary, usually in English, and inevitably invites comparison with the structural component of syllabuses; however, studies of the development of language function in the new language have also been undertaken (Wagner-Gough, 1975; Hatch, 1978). Thirdly, research has been conducted on students in classrooms and on learners in various naturalistic settings, as well as children in bilingual communities. Thus, suggestions for changes in teaching methodology can be made, where appropriate, on the basis of comparisons with naturalistic learning situations.

Comparison of First and Second Language Acquisition

Comparison is frequently invited between the child learning his native tongue and the second language learner. In the previous chapter we saw many error types committed by children learning their first language which might plausibly have been committed by older learners of a second language; the difficulty is identifying the processes leading to those errors in the two situations. Bearing in mind the emphasis on psychological processes in this chapter there are some distinctions to be observed in this comparison, and other comparisons also need to be researched. Language learners differ in the total amount of time they spend on the task. It is difficult, without knowing exactly what language learning is, to estimate how much time a child spends on it; some have argued that it is the preoccupation of his whole waking day, others that he is also busy doing things which are not language, like learning to locomote, to perceive, to solve problems, to think, to interact with parents and peers, to behave morally, to develop his emotional life, and so on. Clearly, those theorists who see a language component in some of these other tasks will hypothesise more time spent on language learning than those who do not.

Estimating the amount of time spent on language learning by a second language learner depends on a second distinction, between informal and formal learning situations. Krashen and Seliger (1975) distinguish between these two kinds of situations in terms of two features, organisation of language exposure and feedback. In formal situations the rules of the language (whether phonological, syntactic, or socio-linguistic) are exposed to the learner in a more or less orderly fashion, in extreme cases, one by one; in informal situations any encounter may potentially involve any combination of the rules of the language. In formal situations, there is opportunity for trial and error and overt feedback to the learner; in informal ones, feedback is less obvious and may be quite absent. However, the time spent on learning may well differ for the second language learners in these two broad categories. It is usual to consider the situation of the child acquiring a first language as more obviously comparable to the second of these alternatives, although there is evidence that adults talking to children do 'engineer' their language (by simplifying the grammar and not using words beyond the children's ken; see Landes, 1975).

The significance of the difference between informal and formal situations is a little difficult to assess. One of the aims of research on second language acquisition is to determine whether the learning processes are the same in their various different circumstances, and to what extent they are similar to those postulated for the child. Many language teachers feel intuitively that the difference between the two kinds of learning situation, at least for adults, is not as significant as the age difference between adulthood and the child's acquisition of the first language. Thus adults' learning processes would be seen as similar in the two categories, and quite different to children's. Be this as it may, the distinction between natural and formal situations may yet be important for adults, as the experiments of Upshur (1968) and Krashen and Seliger (1975) have shown. Adults by and large prefer to learn with a guide to the structure of the language and some predigestion of the learning task, in other words, with a teacher, although retrospective reports (Pickett, 1978) show that the preferred amount of decision-taking by the teacher varies considerably between learners.

A further necessary distinction concerns the description of the progress made by the groups of learners who are to be compared. There has been controversy in L_1 acquisition research on the question of whether children of the same age and language community who are similar in other respects have reached the same stage of language development. In other words, is it meaningful to ask 'Can all children of, say 3 years 2 months, use the past simple tense forms like adults?' The generally accepted answer seems to be that children are as variable in language development as they are in everything else. If age cannot be used as a guide to language development, but language development is fairly regular and consistent between children, then other indices of stages reached should be usable.

The most usual index of development in the first language case has been the mean length of utterance, or MLU, usually measured in morphemes, according to rules originally proposed by R. Brown (1973, p. 78). This measure is useful and apparently valid up to MLU's of about four; after this point patterns of development change. This measure has not been popular with second language researchers, perhaps because older learners' greater memory span blurs the results; however, Larsen-Freeman and Strom (1977) have adapted another length of utterance measure, Kellogg Hunt's minimal terminable unit, or T-unit, as an index of second language development. The T-unit reflects the proportion of simple sentences, conjoining of sentences and subordination of clauses in a stretch of language produced by a learner. It has only been applied to written work.

If the problem is complex in the case of young children, it is even more so in the cases of older children, adolescents and adults learning a second or third language, where the effects of age on speed and order of acquisition are largely unknown. It is at present highly debatable whether the concept of stages of L_2 development comparable to those suggested for L_1 development is meaningful. Stages of L_2 development here refers to stages in the process of acquiring the language and not to stages in progress through a language teaching course.

Error Analysis

A first approximation to a theory of error types – the first division in the field – was suggested by S. P. Corder (1974). He suggested that there are three gross categories of error, namely, (a) pre-systematic, (b) systematic, (c) post-systematic. The terminology used by different writers differs but these three categories have been widely accepted. (a) Pre-systematic errors are those made by a learner while he is groping about trying to understand a new point. (b) Systematic errors are those produced when the learner has formed some conception of the point at issue – a hypothesis – which is, however, wrong in some way. Errors which are related to inaccurate hypotheses will regularly occur. (c) Post-systematic, the third category, covers deviant language forms which occur where previously systematic errors have been corrected – in other words, where there is good reason to believe that a point has been correctly understood and performance has been mainly accurate but the learner has temporarily forgotten it. While this three-way division of errors is eminently reasonable, and highlights the importance of the formation of hypotheses, their refinement and their eventual fixation, it lacks a robust criterion for an outsider who is not privy to the learner's mind to operate the division with. The criterion suggested by Corder was whether self-correction and explanation are possible. With pre-systematic error the learner would not be able to correct or explain the error: he might not even know that an error had been made. He would not be able to correct a systematic error, but he would be able to say why he produced the form in question. He would be able both to correct and to explain a post-systematic error, if it were pointed out. The difficulty with a test such as this is, obviously, that the researcher has to invite the learner to introspect on his own state of mind at the time he produced the erroneous form, and must rely on this evidence – there is no other. Situations are conceivable when an error would be wrongly classified because, for example, the learner was unable to express the hypothesis he had entertained – after all, native speakers can rarely formulate the rules according to which they are speaking, so one cannot assume that non-native speakers will necessarily do any better.

A further, and more controversial, classification of errors was proposed by Selinker (1972). Referring principally to Corder's systematic errors, he mentioned nine different types of systematic error in a list that was not supposed to be exhaustive. These nine types of error are assumed to be related to nine types of learning process or strategy. Selinker was careful to point out that, concerning the word 'strategy', 'a viable definition of it does not seem possible at present' (p. 39). The same, of course, is true of the word 'process'.

The nine types of systematic error suggested by Selinker are as follows:

(1) Language transfer. Items and rules in the learner's version of the new language are directly traceable to the native language. For example, the frequent inability of Arabs to distinguish between /b/ and /p/, or of Japanese between /l/ and /r/.

(2) Transfer of training. The error is directly traceable to some element in the teaching received. Richards (1971) gives the example of an exercise contrasting *permit, allow* and *cause something to do something* with *make something do something* whose effect was to convince a majority of the students that *make something to do something* was the correct English form.

(3) L_2 learning strategy. Selinker suggests that there is frequently a 'tendency on the part of learners to reduce the TL to a simpler system', and that this is a learning strategy.

(4) L_2 communication strategies. A learner may resist the effort of incorporating some of the fine distinctions that native speakers make because he discovers he can either be understood perfectly well without them, or he finds his speech is unacceptably slow and hesitating if he endeavours to produce them exactly. A possible example is the frequent lack of reversion to normal word-order in reported *wh-* (*which, what, who*) questions
     Q: *What is he doing?*
     Reported Q: *She asks what is he doing.*

(5) Overgeneralisation of rules. This process, also referred to as 'ignorance of rule restrictions' (Richards, 1971) is widespread, and an example could be the use of past tense *-ed* morphemes on irregular verbs – *standed, eated.*

(6) Spelling pronunciations, for example, the presence of final /r/ on *farmer*, or medial /l/ in *half.*

(7) Cognate pronunciations, for example, French *athlete* /a/t/l/e/t/. This is however more likely to be language transfer.

(8) Holophrase learning, for example, the classic 'Good morning, sir' to a lady teacher.

(9) Hypercorrection, for example, the German learner's probable overcorrection of English /ou/ as in *go* to /eou/.

Some of the difficulties in classifying systematic errors in this way are immediately apparent. The difference between communication strategies and learning strategies may appear plausible, but when choosing the correct category to place an error in – that is, inferring its cause – the distinction is hardly workable as it stands. Both, clearly, result in simplification of the target language by the learner in order to reduce his cognitive load. However, the simple fact that it is difficult to choose between two categories of error does not necessarily mean that the distinction between them is meaningless. It may mean that the error could equally well be of one or the other type. It should not be supposed that all learners take the same route to the same error. What for one learner is hypercorrection may be a communication strategy for another; what for one learner is ignorance of a rule restriction may be a spelling pronunciation for another. This problem of individual differences has hardly been touched upon in the error analysis literature. Nor should it be assumed that one learner may not, at different times, produce the same error for different reasons. Thus the way an exercise was presented may have taught him something false: a case of transfer of training; but the error may have persisted after independent contact with native speakers because it did not seriously impair communication: a case of a communication strategy.

Selinker proposed a global distinction between the first five and the last four of the above processes or strategies. This distinction was between errors that were fossilisable, that is, were practically ineradicable, and errors which were not. Processes leading to fossilisation of errors were thought to be central processes, since those applications or runs of them that did not lead to error did, presumably, lead to equally ineradicable accuracies. According to Selinker, the first five of the error types illustrated central processes in this sense.

Another difficulty with these categories concerns the preoccupation with error itself. It is quite reasonable to attempt to describe the set of rules that produces systematic errors in terms of some learning processes; but it is ultimately a desire to describe how language is learned rather than not learned which motivates the operation. Therefore it should be possible to translate these processes into explanations of correct language performance, as an alternative to the rote-learning hypothesis. For this purpose, some of the processes are easier to translate than others.

Elicitation Approaches

Production

Dulay and Burt (1974), taking a leaf out of R. Brown's first language acquisition research (1973), experimented with children aged between 8 and 11 who, already speaking their native Spanish or Chinese, were attending English-speaking schools in the USA. They were receiving some English language instruction in the schools but many different textbooks and courses were in use. Dulay and Burt's experimental method was to show the children some pictures and ask questions designed to elicit certain types of language form. This method has been standardised and published as the bilingual syntax measure (BSM). They were looking for correct usage of eleven little grammatical words and endings, called 'functors', which, as Brown had already shown, appear in a fairly consistent order in native American children after a certain stage of language acquisition has been reached. Whenever a child answering the researcher's questions used a sentence in which an adult would be obliged to use one of these functors, he or she was scored right or wrong on this 'obligatory occasion' according to whether he/she used the functor correctly or not. If the child performed correctly on two out of three occasions he/she was assumed to know that functor. The performance of each child on each functor was then compared to see whether it could be said that at some criterion level of 90 per cent, some functors were prerequisite to others: that is, whether any children could use function X if they had not already learnt function Y. They found that the eleven functors fell into three groups, within which there were no great differences, but between which there were: virtually no children could use functors in group III if they could not use functors in group II, and hardly any children could use functors in group II if they could not use those forms in group I. In this manner, Dulay and Burt found a natural hierarchy. The functors grouped as follows:

I   pronoun case
II   copula, auxiliary, plural -s, continuous -ing, articles
III possessive 's, regular and irregular past tense, 3rd person -s, plural -es.

There was some ordering within groups II and III.

This was a cross-sectional study; the implication of these results is that any child in this age-range will go through this sequence in learning English, but of course this still has to be tested in longitudinal studies of individual children. We will examine this comparison in more detail later. It is for this reason that the authors claimed that there was a natural hierarchy of acquisition that appeared to be controlled by the one factor common to all the children: the English language. Variation due to the children's different mother tongues or different English courses at school was negligible.

Interpretation of results like the above is not easy. R. Brown (1973) had shown that in the case of native learners a quite different hierarchy was obtained, one which was predictable on either or both of two explanations: linguistic (transformational) complexity or semantic complexity. Since the foreign children go through a different sequence, these explanations cannot hold. Nevertheless, some explanation in terms of the language input and the rule-construction process might be found.

Several other studies have used the cross-sectional method to establish orders of difficulty for morphemes, for example, Bailey, Madden and Krashen (1974), using the BSM (bilingual syntax measure) test, and Fathman (1975) using another test designed on somewhat different principles, the SLOPE (Second Language Oral Production Examination) test.

Rosansky (1977) has raised fundamental objections, however, to this whole approach of using elicited data. She points out that there are two dangerous assumptions: (1) elicited data are a valid measure of spontaneous productive ability, (2) cross-sectional data are equivalent to longitudinal data. In her research she has shown that there are good reasons for not accepting either of these assumptions. The first assumption is challenged by the finding that the morpheme acquisition order established by the BSM does not correlate with orders discovered by observing spontaneous speech, either for native children (Porter, 1977, quoted by Rosansky) or for non-native children (Rosansky, 1977). Furthermore the results of the BSM test seem to be highly task-specific: in other words, it seems to give idiosyncratic results. The second assumption is challenged by her failure to find significant correlation between the two types of data, for individual subjects.

Comprehension

Experiments have also been conducted to investigate problems of comprehension experienced by L_2 acquirers. Cook (1973), in one of his experiments, has attempted to compare adult learners of EFL with native acquirers of English, learning the correct identification of the agent in pairs of sentences where the agent is not overtly marked. He controlled for the difference between natural L_1 and formal L_2 exposure by selecting an element of the language that was not explicitly covered in the course of instruction. This was the difference between

> The wolf is hard to bite
> The wolf is willing to bite

Cromer (1970) had already shown that children follow a consistent sequence in learning to interpret these sentences (see Chapter 7, p. 105). Cook's foreign adults went through exactly the same stages, but these were related to length of English study at home and abroad. This evidence appears to show that, at the very least, there are some parts of English grammar which foreign adults and native children may learn by similar psychological processes, whatever those processes may be. One interesting feature of this experiment is the fact that the foreign adults recapitulated the children's stages despite already having experience, in their many native tongues, of similar, opaque surface structures; this knowledge does not appear to have helped them.

As the fourth illustration of the elicitation approach, a piece of research by d'Anglejan and Tucker (1975) gives another insight into how the comparison between foreign adults at different stages and native children can be conducted. They set out to discover the extent to which the pattern of difficulty of certain verb phrases discovered by C. S. Chomsky (1969) in children aged 5 to 10 was also repeated in adult EFL learners. They compared two groups of adult learners, rated as beginners and advanced by the language school placement test, on four types of sentence, all of which involved identification of the agent of some action. The experimental task was the same as that used by Cook: answering a simple comprehension question.

Chomsky had shown that, for certain verb types, verbal complements in which the agent was the nearest noun phrase on the left of the verb were understood at an earlier age than complements in which the agent was further away. This grammatical difference is an instance of a very general principle known as the minimal distance principle (MDP). There are far fewer occasions where this principle is lawfully abandoned than when it applies (see Chapter 7, p. 105).

In three of d'Anglejan and Tucker's conditions, one half of the sentences were in a form which obeyed the MDP; the other half disobeyed it (the (b) sentences here):

2	Presented Sentence	Experimental Question
(a)	*Jim asked Peter to read his letter.*	*Who will read the letter?*
(b)	*Jim promised Peter to read his letter.*	*Who will read the letter?*

3   (with pictures)
  (a)   *Which picture shows the boy telling the girl which shoes to wear?*
  (b)   *Which picture shows the boy asking the girl which shoes to wear?*

The results of their study were that the adult French-speaking learners appeared to approach this task in the same way as did Chomsky's children. There could be several reasons for this, for example: the second language learners used the operating principles of language acquisition as the native children might have; or, the second language learners were confused about the English structures because the underlying semantic structure is not overtly marked as it is in French, with the prepositions *à* and *de*. So far there has been no experimental test of these two possibilities.

Longitudinal Studies

A popular research strategy has been to follow a learner's pattern of development through a long time-period, recording samples of language and concurrent behaviour and interaction at frequent and regular intervals. Using this approach, some interesting regular features have been discovered.

Prefabricated utterances

Several pieces of research have confirmed the idea that learners at an early stage use sequences of words which they produce by rote, that is, without knowing the full grammar that native speakers presumably use to construct them. Such sequences are typically correct in internal form but do not vary with syntactic or situational context. They have been called 'routines', 'prefabricated utterances', 'holophrases'. Their function, apart from their literal meaning, is to maintain conversation and keep the communication channel open. An example from Hakuta (1976) was given in Chapter 3 (pp. 35–6) when discussing apparent decrement in performance in connection with learning plateaux (Uguisu: *I know how to do it*). As the learner's knowledge of underlying grammar catches up with the apparent grammatical sophistication of the routine phrase, there is a period of misuse and error. Eventually the construction can be used with all the necessary morphological changes for different circumstances. R. Clark (1974) has shown that a similar process occurs in first language acquisition. Wagner-Gough (1975) presents an interesting example of an imitation process which could be the first stage of the formation of such routines. Her subject, Homer, a speaker of Farsi and Assryian of nearly 6 years of age, when giving affirmative answers to questions addressed to him would typically repeat the question with a falling intonation:

J: *Is Misty a cat?*

Homer: *Is Misty a cat.*   (= Yes, Misty is a cat.)

Later the same word order was used in Homer's own questions.

Negatives

The development of the English negative has attracted a good deal of attention. Cancino, Rosansky and Schumann (1978) looked at the learning of English by six Spanish speakers, two children, two adolescents, and two adults. They found a consistent developmental sequence. The pattern can be summarised as follows:

Stage 1	*no* + verb	e.g.	*I no understand*
Stage 2	*don't* + verb	e.g.	*I don't can explain*
			I don't hear
Stage 3	auxiliary or modal + negative	e.g.	*You can't tell her*
			We couldn't do anything
Stage 4	analysed forms of *don't*	e.g.	*I didn't have a light*
	Stage 1 disappears		*It doesn't make any difference*
			(Cancino *et al.*, 1978)

Stage 1 occurs in first language acquisition; it could also be interference from Spanish ([yo] *no entiendo*). The remaining three stages bear a striking resemblance to the sequence chosen for several structuralist EFL texts, in particular the use of unanalysed *don't* (but in the context of imperatives and classroom instructions), and the introduction of *can* and *can't* as modal auxiliaries before the full variety of auxiliary *do* forms. Presumably the motivation for the latter point in both cases is to develop a meaningful auxiliary with the correct word-order before a dummy *do* which only carries tense and number marking. The modals *can*, *can't* and *couldn't* have Spanish equivalents with the same word-order, but the *do* auxiliary does not occur in Spanish.

Wode's (1976) report on a German learner of English shows a similar sequence, but with interesting differences:

Stage IIb	*no* + verb	e.g.	*No play baseball*
Stage III	verb + negative	e.g.	*John go not to school*
	modal auxiliary + negative		*I can no play with Kenny*
Stage IIIb			*I didn't see*
Stage IV	analysed *do* negative	e.g.	*don't tell nobody*

(adapted from Wode, 1976, p. 17, table 4)

Wode's stage IIb looks very like Cancino *et al.*'s stage 1, his stage III has elements of their stages 2 and 3, and his stage IV is much like their stage 4, particularly if one includes his stage IIIb. The appearance of the modal *can* before the auxiliary *do* is again clear. However, there is also a strong effect of German word-order, in which the negative element follows the verb (*John geht nicht zur Schule*).

Interrogatives

This is another area in which considerable research effort has been expended. Question forms have always been thought difficult to teach as they involve inversion and the auxiliary *do*, and classroom situations which force the students to ask rather than only to answer questions.

First, questions that only require a *yes* or *no* answer in English are usually formed by inversion of subject and copula or by pre-posing *do*:

Is he a painter?

Do you smoke?

This kind of question form usually develops early, with two discernible stages (Cancino *et al.*, 1978), the first, a simple affirmative word-order with rising intonation, the second, adding inversion. However, the pre-posing of the auxiliary may not always in fact be a true inversion at first. Cancino *et al.* point out that the preposed *do* for their Spanish speakers may simply be a dummy marker of the question form rather than a real, modifiable auxiliary. Ervin-Tripp (1974, fn. 7) quotes a student of hers, Milgrom, who noticed that Hebrew-speaking children learning English used *is* and *do* in front of nucleus sentences where Hebrew has a question-marking form:

> *Is it he is singing a song?*
>
> *Do you can tell me what is the time?*

One might expect a similar pattern of development from French-speaking learners, whose language can form *yes/no* questions with *est-ce que* ...? (*is it that* + nucleus?).

Secondly, questions that are introduced by a question marker in English, like *what?*, *how?*, *who?*, and so on, are attempted early in the learning sequence in naturalistic settings, whereas in school syllabuses they tend to be introduced later. Hatch (1974) showed that in large numbers of studies the *wh-* question forms were tacked on to the front of utterances before any of the necessary syntactic changes were known, like the use of the copula, tense-marking, or the *do* auxiliary. However, the sounds spelled *what's*, *who's* are often learnt as alternative forms, without knowledge of the contracted copula which the native grammar identifies. In later stages, learners begin introducing auxiliary inversion and then have to distinguish between simple and embedded questions. This can lead to a stage identified by Hakuta (1976), among others, where a copula form appears twice:

> *I don't know where is this is.*

I have also noticed this doubling with speakers of Arabic.

This example of data from longitudinal studies of patterns of development show how this method can reveal patterns of change over time which are most interesting to compare with existing and frequently used teaching syllabuses. Because most of the subjects in these studies were either too young, or too old, or too remote, to attend normal EFL classes, and were picking the language up in naturalistic settings, one can discount the possibility that similarities with existing syllabuses came about through direct contact. Nevertheless, it seems clear that in some cases, such as the order of appearance of *can* and *do* as auxiliaries, the belief that there is some intrinsic order of difficulty here is confirmed by several studies. While there do appear to be some patterns of development that are similar for students of many different mother tongues, and are therefore probably not due to interference from those languages, it is also clear that there are quite important deviations from the general patterns which are due to contrasts between the first and the second languages. One fairly concrete result to be expected from this kind of work therefore is a set of probabilistic guidelines for classifying developmental and contrastive errors, that is, errors due to intrinsic complications of the new language and errors due to contrast with the mother tongue.

Conversational Analysis

Recently another research strategy has been developed, somewhat paralleling the research on adults talking to children and children's peer-group talk: the analysis of conversation between native speaker and non-native learner. The majority of this work (see Hatch, 1976) has been concerned with conversations outside a recognisable, or traditional, teaching situation, and there have been very few studies of foreign language conversation in the classroom. Also, most of the work has been conducted using children as the non-native learners, and it is perhaps not surprising that in this situation very similar results are found to those obtained in the study of first language acquisition discourse. Some of the results are very interesting. Conversational processes have been found which are similar to those from which a child may derive the structure of his native language. For example, Hatch, quoting data from an unpublished thesis by Young, claims that normal processes of attention-getting and topic nomination accounts for sentences like 'this (noun)' in the language of young L_2 learners. Her argument rests on the assumption that in the following conversation the two utterances by the child are linked by their function, despite the second simply being a repetition of the content word used by the adult:

	Utterance	Function
Non-native child:	*that*	pointing: topic nomination
Native speaker adult:	*It's a truck*	topic identification and acceptance
Non-native child:	*truck*	agreement?

(adapted from Hatch, 1976, p. 52)

It is further assumed that these two utterances are in fact one interrupted utterance, and that this is the origin for the child's ability to produce both utterances together, for example, 'that truck'.

In Scollon's (1976) terms, the series of interrupted utterances are 'vertical', and a single utterance uttered as a unit of more or less complexity is 'horizontal': the assumption is that horizontal utterances derive from vertical ones. Scollon, working in the first language field, has argued that one of the lessons that children learn from conversations is the ordering of constituents in a complex utterance because of the order of the questions which the adult asks to get the child to elaborate what he is trying to say. Since the child produces the relevant words in the order the adult has asked the questions, and the adult has asked the questions in the order their answers would have been in the adult syntax, so the child's interrupted vertical utterance becomes the basis for later correct word order in horizontal utterances. This theory has not been tested at all widely and there is neither a volume of empirical evidence for it nor compelling reasons to justify its assumptions; nevertheless it remains plausible until proved wrong, as all other theories. Whether or not similar conversational processes can be shown (a) to take place in the case of older learners of a foreign language and (b) if so, whether they are the locus of learning, is a matter for future research. Older learners are going to have far more subtle expectations about the language, the situation, the topic, the conversational rules and the interlocution; and the interlocutor, whether an official teacher or not, is going to have equally subtle and differentiated expectations about the capabilities (and previous knowledge) of the learner. Generalisation, therefore, from any one piece of research in this area is not valid. However, the principle that learners learn by conversing in the language is an ancient one and is now ripe for some detailed analysis. The results of the analysis may tell teachers which of their ways of talking with individual learners or with a class are most likely actually to promote learning.

Some Implications for Language Teaching

Since this whole research area is comparatively new, it is not possible to conclude with a recipe of practical recommendations for the classroom, founded in an established base of theory and results. The exact usefulness of the findings of error analysis and experimentation which have been selectively outlined above is difficult to state, precisely because there is no theory of the psychological processes of second language learning as yet. For example, we need a theory of learning processes to systematise the labelling of errors and to relate them to the evolution of correct performance, and we need a coherent theory which will relate investigations of the development of grammar, vocabulary, pronunciation and communicative function to each other. Nevertheless, in the absence of such a theory there are at least two major questions arising which are of immediate concern to teachers and course writers.

The first of these is the possibility that error patterns and consistent orders of acquisition of elements reflect some natural sequence of acquisition of a foreign language, an internal syllabus, which is governed in some way by the language to be learnt and not by external circumstances of exposure, method of instruction, and so on, and may or may not be related in detail to the unfolding of language which appears to take place in first language learning. The evidence for such an internal syllabus is increasing, but it is by no means conclusive. Nevertheless, if it is proven, language instruction will have to face the problem of providing courses and instructional exercises which aid rather than hinder its operation. Whether the solution will be to sequence the exposure to the language in accordance with the natural sequence, or to reduce the importance of sequencing material as an instructional device and give full rein to the learner's active participation, is a matter for experiment. Obviously, allowing the student's language to evolve in the way documented for learning in naturalistic settings, or rewriting syllabuses to incorporate some of the findings in the order of acquisition given above (for example, the early, and syntactically ill-formed use of *wh-* question forms) implies a quite new attitude to classroom language and accuracy. Utterances would be evaluated for their communicative success and their progress checked against some normative set of developmental stages; but the students would be without the motivation that is supposedly conferred by the knowledge that each lesson contains only authentic language which can be put to use immediately, outside the confines of the classroom. Of course, that disadvantage might be outweighed by the advantage of a reasonable degree of fluency.

The second immediate problem that arises is that of the teacher's treatment of error. It is clear that avoidance of error is impossible; tolerance of error may be unproductive, but prediction and diagnosis of error may be all-important. Prediction of error can be the basis for a systematic 'guided discovery' method of teaching; the most instructive errors can be prepared and profitably utilised. A language exercise which sets traps for the learner (Dakin, 1973) in a carefully controlled manner needs to be designed on the basis of what types of error are the most profitable for eventual (and rapid) success. Diagnosis of error every teacher has to perform many times during the course of a lesson; Corder's qualitative distinction between gross error types enables the teacher to decide which errors are formative and which are not, and thus on what basis to design corrective treatment, if any. Studies of error types and natural sequences will furthermore indicate what the underlying cause of a particular error may have been. Teachers should, obviously, beware that their own treatment of error does not itself provoke further unprofitable errors. It has been claimed (Allwright, 1975) that this danger is far greater than had previously been supposed.

Studies of second language learning have the potential of giving course writers and teachers direct evidence of how people learn languages, which, coupled with an analysis of how various teaching techniques work, can eventually lead to a systematic and rich account of the teaching–learning process to be embodied in new types of language course and thus result in more successful learners.

Chapter 9

Individual Differences

A great deal of the work referred to in the previous chapters has tended to assume, if only for clarity's sake, that the discovery, trait, or phenomenon in question is true of all humans, or at least of all humans in that particular situation. But, of course, this is most unlikely. We do not all behave or think identically. All teachers know that some of their students will cope easily with the learning material and activities and some will not. Some will succeed and others will not. Many of the differences in achievement will be due to circumstances like sickness, administrative problems, changing schools, and so on, but many will be attributable to inherent characteristics of the learner or teacher. Such different characteristics may be totally idiosyncratic and, if this is the case, no provision except human understanding by the teacher can be made for them and no generalisations made about them. However, there may be regular features about these individual differences such that they fall into broad groups or categories, and the following two chapters introduce some of these categories. Specifically, this chapter discusses the categories of intelligence, aptitude, learning style, and personality, while the following one takes a close look at the concept of motivation.

Individual characteristics of learners may be directly or indirectly related to achievement in foreign language learning. For example, motivation may be directly and positively related, as the higher the degree of motivation the harder the learner will work and the longer he or she will persist. Cognitive style variables may be only indirectly related, as it is possible that their connection with student achievement is the result of a favourable or unfavourable match with the teacher's methodology. Quite a lot of research effort has been devoted to elucidating what kinds of learning characteristics do appear to be related to success in learning foreign languages, and in what way they are related.

If this research effort does reach conclusions on the existence of individual student characteristics that are favourably related to language learning, the language teacher needs to know how this knowledge can be used. Here we will draw out six possible strategies, but reserve discussion of them until after the evidence for and against some suggested relevant factors has been reviewed. Basically, given general information about individual differences, teachers can

(1) do nothing different, as the variables involved are so complex and the effects relatively small;
(2) use such knowledge in the diagnosis of learning problems;
(3) select only students who have the demonstrated relevant qualities;
(4) select a method which is known to match the kind of learner they have;
(5) train the students to adopt the behaviour characteristics of good language learners;
(6) only teach students whose learning characteristics match their own in some way.

Whichever option or combination of options a teacher selects will depend on a number of factors, including ideological ones to do with conceptions of education and the desirable degree of learner-centredness of teaching. We return to these options after discussing some kinds of relevant student characteristics.

Intelligence

The nature of intelligence and its relation to educational decisions has, of course, been a matter of controversy and heated debate for many years. Intelligence tests were originally devised to measure the quality of brightness or intellectual capacity that was thought to underlie school achievement; the original tests devised by Binet in France, Burt in England, and Stanford and Terman in the USA (which shared many common features) were designed to give a measure which was not affected by actual learning, that is, in a sense, to measure the capacity rather than the contents of the mind. Therefore many of the crucial items in tests were somewhat abstract and quasi-mathematical problems. Furthermore it was assumed that such a capacity would be unequally distributed in the population as are height and other physical characteristics.

Research on intelligence testing has focused on the predictive power of the tests (whether they do provide an adequate indication of future scholastic achievement); the origin of the results on a test (whether differences in measured intelligence are contaminated by recent learning, or are attributable to heredity or early infant experience); the distribution of the scores (unequal distribution, specifically the so-called normal distribution, is still assumed, in which there is a clustering of the majority of the scores in a small range round the midpoint and progressively fewer scores towards either extreme); and the nature and development of the characteristic intellectual quality of which the scores are the outward reflection.

Intelligence tests, whose results are conventionally quoted as either mental age (that is, the average chronological age of the total population having a particular score) or as intelligence quotient (IQ) (that is, the ratio of mental age to chronological age, usually multiplied by 100 to get rid of the decimal point), are usually found to have a reasonably useful power of predicting success in school subjects. One would not expect it to be very high in any particular subject, because of the general nature of the concept, and no school subject relies more heavily on it than any other. Argument has raged for some time about the use of intelligence tests in education, centring mainly on three issues. These include the difficulty of specifying further the nature of intelligence, which has resulted in attitudes like 'Intelligence is what intelligence tests measure' which is understandable as an operational definition from the psychometric point of view but not, usually, from that of parents and teachers who would like to know more about cognitive functioning. The second issue has been the justifiability of using IQ to select pupils for particular kinds of secondary education, especially in view of the problem of the late developer, who appears not to have adequate IQ at age 11 but does at age 13 or 14, when the choice of schooling and thereby occupational opportunities in later life may have already been taken. The third has been the problem of the self-fulfilling prophecy, in which teachers who are given IQs for the children they teach appear to treat the children differentially, thus ensuring that academic success follows as predicted by the IQ ratings (for a full account of both sides of this argument, see Sperry, 1972, pt 2). However, in addition to these general problems, the relevance of measured intelligence to foreign language learning is questionable for more specific reasons.

First, intelligence does not appear to be an important factor in first language acquisition. Lenneberg (1964) showed that as long as mentally retarded children achieve the minimal degree of intellectual functioning that is concomitant with upright gait and bowel control, some language skills such as naming will develop (which is more than the highest apes in the natural state), and children of not much more mental development use recognisable grammatical organisation. Intelligence does play a part in later school life, where it predicts the development of fluent writing skills. If IQ is not strongly related to the emergence of the first language, then it has to be demonstrated that it is related to second language learning; it cannot be assumed.

Secondly, measured intelligence is difficult to separate from first language knowledge at school age, since most intelligence tests are conducted through the medium of language, and many contain specifically linguistic items such as 'odd man out' questions (for example, *Which is the odd man out: goose, duck, table, bison?*). This tendency is probably a relic of the earliest tests, developed at the beginning of the century, since when a large amount of research effort has been devoted to the very complex question of the relationship between cognitive and linguistic development. There have been efforts to develop language-free intelligence tests such as the performance scale of the Wechsler Intelligence Scale for Children (WISC), but even in these the possibility that language is used as a mediator in concept formation and as a regulator of behaviour in solving problems cannot be eliminated.

Thirdly, intelligence may not be related to language learning as such, but to the ability to profit from certain kinds of instruction. It seems likely that, in a natural situation with a strong motivation to learn, people of both above average and below average IQ will do so; but the same may not be true in the classroom situation. Pimsleur, Mosberg and Morrison (1962) showed that IQ did correlate with school learning of French in US schools, but only to a low level (as for other subjects); but Chastain (1969) found that the correlation existed for students taught by cognitive-code type methods, but was insignificant for students taught by audio-lingual methods. Thus it is possible that IQ predicts success in most school subjects including foreign languages when the teaching style is rather similar in each (for example, expounding rules, examination of instances, teacher explanations, some rote-learning), but not when a strange method is used. More recently, Genesee (1978) found, again with French, but with English-speaking Canadian students in a bilingual French immersion programme in Montreal, that rated IQ correlated quite highly with scholastic skills as measured by knowledge tests, in particular a standard pencil-and-paper *teste du rendement en français* and a reading test, (and a mathematics test as well), but not at all with native speakers' ratings of the students' communicative abilities in French. Thus IQ may only be relevant for certain skills which are particularly redolent of school learning and do not necessarily reflect desirable aims for language teaching.

Aptitude

If intelligence is of questionable relevance to language learning, perhaps there exists a specific aptitude or talent for the activity which not everybody possesses – an ear for languages. Research on this topic has tended to follow the psychometric approach, developing batteries of tests which correlate highly with achievement, low with each other, and low with other tests such as IQ. The nature of the aptitude is then interpreted from the kinds of test items that survive the period of test development as valid and reliable predictors of achievement. Two broad categories of ability feature in the published tests of aptitude: language knowledge and auditory ability.

Language knowledge was found by Carroll and Sapon (1959), Pimsleur (1968a) and Green (1975) to be important. Carroll and Sapon's Modern Language Aptitude Test (MLAT) includes a test of L_1 grammatical sensitivity, requiring students to spot words fulfilling similar syntactic functions in different sentences. Pimsleur's Language Aptitude Battery (LAB) has a job sample test which actually requires the students to learn a limited grammatical manipulation in an exotic language. The MLAT has a test of vocabulary learning in an exotic language, and a test of disguised spelling which might gauge the ability to see that words in related languages are cognate forms (for example, *medium, mezzo, Mitte, mahdya*). The LAB measures knowledge of infrequent words in the native language. The subtests in these batteries which measure language knowledge in these ways (called variously verbal intelligence or verbal ability) are found to be very good predictors of success in learning in the school and college situations they were developed to serve.

Gardner and Lambert (1959) discovered that in their population of school learners of French in bi-cultural Montreal, verbal intelligence (measured by an early version of the MLAT) was one of the two most powerful traits associated with achievement. The other was orientation to language learning, a motivational trait which will be discussed more fully in the next chapter. Pimsleur's LAB contains a measure of motivational intensity, a short questionnaire, which is included in the total aptitude score. While this addition undoubtedly enhances Pimsleur's battery as a predictive instrument, it is convenient here to separate the concepts of aptitude, or talent, and motivation. Aptitude generally refers to a disposition to be able to do something well, motivation to a willingness to do it.

Both of these published aptitude tests incorporate an auditory component. Carroll and Sapon test what they label 'phonetic coding ability' with two techniques, a spoken number recognition task (which, using an artificial language, may also test inductive learning ability), and a spoken syllable recognition task (for example, *Underline the word you hear: tik, tiyk, tis, tiys*). Pimsleur's test devotes nearly half of the total testing time to two auditory tests. His test of sound symbol association uses the same principle as Carroll's phonetic script test, which is ultimately based on the ability to extend knowledge of the spelling system of (American) English to phonologically possible non-existent words. His sound discrimination test requires the candidate to learn three similar-sounding, but not identical, words, in an exotic language (Ewe). He then has to pick out which of the words occurs in sentences spoken in that language. Some of the items rely on phonetic distinctions which may occur in English but do not distinguish between words meaning different things, that is to say they are phonemic in Ewe but not in English. Pimsleur, Sundland and MacIntyre (1964) reported that in an investigation of school pupils who were not achieving as well in French as they were in their other subjects, the auditory tests of the LAB were the only components on which these pupils were significantly less able than the other pupils. They concluded that auditory ability was the most important single factor in language aptitude. However, this conclusion has to be treated with caution, as subtests of a battery such as this are rather short to be reliable enough to base far-reaching conclusions on.

Furthermore, using an aptitude measure as a diagnostic test during the language learning experience incurs the risk that the scores will reflect the experience rather than pre-existing, inherent characteristics.

These types of test were chosen specifically because they correlated highly with achievement and were relatively independent of each other and other available measures such as IQ. As we have seen, Pimsleur (1968b) argued that the language-specific tests gave the best prediction, when taken in conjunction with achievement in other subjects and a quick measure of interest. The explanation of aptitude that can be derived from the tests is, however, only a partial one. Interpretation of the tests and their interactions gives a set of abilities which they are gauging, but these abilities do not bear any obvious and simple relationship to cognitive processes discovered by normal experimental methods, except perhaps to immediate memory. Therefore it is difficult to know how a figure representing the aptitude of a candidate for language learning can be used to adapt that experience for the candidate, except as an imperfect indication of possible success, assuming the candidate and the learning situation are comparable to the original reference group and situation tested by the test developers.

Cognitive Style

In the early 1960s there was an upsurge of interest in individual characteristics that did not seem to be part of general intelligence, nor specific to particular subject matters, but which reflected systematic differences in the way individuals preferred to approach learning and problem-solving tasks. These were generally called learning, or cognitive, styles. Messick (1970) described them in general terms: 'Cognitive styles are, for the most part, information-processing habits. They are characteristic modes of operation which, although not necessarily completely independent of content, tend to function across a variety of content areas.' Their identification and etiology have been a matter of fierce debate among researchers; the nine types cited by Messick are not necessarily independent, and in several cases suspicion exists that different groups of researchers used different labels and different tests for traits that seem substantially identical. The educational importance of cognitive style may have been exaggerated; the original thrust of research concentrated on the possible interaction between individual characteristics and teaching methods (method A might be good for some pupils, method B for others), but other research has cast doubt on the feasibility of establishing such interaction in general terms (Bracht and Glass, 1972).

Here, however, we are concerned with a more limited question, that of the relation, if any, of learning style to language learning. For example, it may be the case that a certain learning style is better adapted to learning languages than its obverse or another style. Instead of an interaction between style and method (which, of course, may still exist), there might be an interaction between style and subject matter. For example, there has long been a feeling among teachers and learners alike that being eye-minded is a distinct advantage in language learning. Thus many people seem to believe that it is easier to learn languages if you are good at imagining the way the words are spelled and at visualising what is being said in the foreign language. Such people often want much written support and do not believe they can learn words from their sound alone. This kind of preference for one sense mode is perhaps in contrast with the results on auditory ability mentioned in the context of aptitude. If eye-mindedness were established as a valid and relevant individual difference, it would be an example of a style–subject matter interaction. In fact not very much work has been performed on these modality preferences; Chastain (1969) failed to find a significant correlation with success in either cognitive or audio-lingual teaching.

Naiman, Fröhlich and Stern (1975) chose to investigate the relationship between some cognitive style measures and language learning as part of their study, 'The good language learner'. The only style measure to show a definite association in their study was the dimension known as field independence v. field dependence. This trait is described by Witkin (quoted by Messick, 1970) as 'an analytical, in contrast to a global, way of perceiving [which] entails a tendency to experience items as discrete from their backgrounds and reflects ability to overcome the influence of an embedding context'. The trait is normally assessed with a test involving locating a previously seen simple geometric figure within a complex figure designed to contain it. The score is the mean amount of time required for twenty-four such items.

Naiman *et al.*, found that in the highest school classes they investigated, grade 12 in the Toronto (Canada) public school system, field independence correlated highly with both of their proficiency measures, a sentence imitation task and a listening comprehension task. The language being learnt was French. Thus the good language learners had an analytic approach to their subject, as described above. In the lower grades there was no effect. They also found that the field-independent, analytic learners committed characteristic types of errors on the sentence imitation task. The analytic learners were more likely to omit small items of the sentence to be repeated than large chunks, as in A1 below:

Repeat: *La maman de mon ami m'a donné son beau manteau rouge.*
A1 :   *La maman de mon ami a donné son beau manteau rouge.*
A2 :   *La maman de mon ami.*

whereas field-dependent, global learners were more likely to omit larger chunks, as in A2. Analytic learners were also less likely than global learners to commit certain substitutions in imitation, for example, in repeating the sentence :

Repeat: *Hier quelqu'un nous a raconté une belle histoire.*

The substitution of *avons* for *a* as if *nous* were the subject and not the pre-posed object pronoun was less likely from field-independent learners.

However, although it is tempting to conclude that field independence is an inherently advantageous cognitive style for language learning there is an alternative explanation. This association between an analytic cognitive style and good language learning could have been the product of the school system. It only appeared in grade 12, and many of the students in public full-time education in that grade would probably have been preparing for university or college entrance. It seems possible that such students might have been encouraged to adopt an analytic turn of mind as part of their preparation for tertiary education. If the teaching methods were progressively favouring the field-independent, analytic style, perhaps disadvantaging the global, field-dependent style, then one would expect an improvement in the performance of some of the weaker field-dependent students and a corresponding worsening of some of the better field-dependent students. By grade 12 the association found between cognitive style and language learning could be established. Until this alternative possible explanation is ruled out by a close examination of teaching methods and the teachers' assumptions one cannot conclude that there is an inherent predisposition for field-independent learners to succeed in learning foreign languages.

Other measures of cognitive style that have been suggested as possibly having an association with language learning include

broad v. narrow categorising
reflectivity v. impulsivity
levelling v. sharpening [see Chapter 5, p. 69]
belief congruence v. contradiction.

(H. D. Brown, 1973)

Breadth of categorisation refers to a tendency to include many items together in the same broad class, or to categorise narrowly and exclude some items. In relation to language learning this implies a consistent preference for either overgeneralisation or under-use of analogy. However, although such differences in style are intuitively plausible, Naiman *et al.* failed to find a correlation between Pettigrew's category width test and their measures of achievement, or any particular error pattern.

Reflectivity versus impulsivity is usually measured by the time taken for the first response on Kagan's matching familiar figure test. A picture of a familiar object is shown by itself and then must be found from among a collection, all except one of which differs in some detail. A reflective person tends to review all the evidence before making a choice, an impulsive one gambles after a quick and probably partial review of the alternatives. This bears some affinity with Bruner, Goodnow and Austin's (1956) strategies for problem-solving, particularly with their simultaneous scanning and focus gambling strategies. Unfortunately no test of the relationship between this cognitive style and language learning has yet been carried out. One could hypothesise that while impulsive learners might be more successful in naturalistic or perhaps communicative language learning situations, since they are more willing to sacrifice accuracy for speed of response and therefore, perhaps, participation in conversation, reflective learners might succeed in more formal learning environments where there may be an admonition to 'think before you speak'.

Research on cognitive style in education has been hampered by conceptual and methodological difficulties. One of these is the question of the extent to which these tests are really only measuring partial aspects of general intelligence; it is undeniable that in several cases one pole of the dimension corresponds to a socially or academically valued characteristic, and therefore it is not surprising that a correlation with school achievement is obtained (for example, analytic thought; conceptual differentiation; sharpening of details in memory; high tolerance for unconventional experiences), and IQ also correlates with these by design. Another is the question, already touched on, of whether obtained results are the reflections of inherent and stable characteristics or the effects of learning experiences. Another question is the status of the style preferences as traits of personality, and it is to this wider perspective that we now turn.

Personality

It is clear that one can view individual preferences in cognitive functioning as an aspect of personality, particularly those that involve personal value systems such as the fourth mentioned above, belief congruence, which refers to an individual's willingness to entertain beliefs or ways of thought that differ from his own, at least for the purpose of arguments or learning. However, personality study has usually been concerned with value systems as such, attitudes, social behaviour, and emotional reactions. Teachers, students and researchers have long been interested in the question of whether certain personality traits were advantageous, or the reverse, for learning second languages.

Naiman et al. (1975) administered the extroversion scale of the Eysenck Personality Inventory (EPI) to their school populations in Ontario to test the common assumption that outgoing, other-directed talkative personalities are more successful at language learning than their introspective and socially ill-at-ease counterparts. They found no correlation between the answers to the questionnaire and their criterion achievement measures in French, listening comprehension and sentence imitation, but they commented that the questionnaire replies also failed to agree with their own impressions gained from classroom observation and interviews. They concluded that they were not satisfied with the validity of the EPI as a measure of extroverted tendencies. However, it may have been the case that their criterion measures were simply not sensitive to the relevant kinds of performance. Cohen (1977), in an extensive review paper, quotes an unpublished study by Rossier (1975), who did find a positive correlation between the EPI (in Spanish) and a pictorial stimulus test of oral fluency in English, among fifty grade 12 Spanish-speaking ESL students (IQ, time spent studying in the USA and grade point average were controlled for in this study). It seems plausible that extroverts are more likely to perform better on tests of oral proficiency than on tests of imitation or listening comprehension, if there is any truth in the correlation between this trait and language learning.

However, extroversion/introversion is not just a matter of attitude and opinions as measured by a specific questionnaire. Cohen (1977) points out that three of the four traits isolated by Tucker, Hamayan and Genesee (1976) as related to success speaking French in an immersion programme are commonly associated with the popular conception of extroversion, namely, assertiveness, emotional stability and adventuresomeness. Questionnaires do not elicit behaviour, merely opinions and self-ratings. Naiman et al. (1975) also lumped together a number of behavioural measures from their classroom observations into a composite classroom personality factor, and found that this did relate significantly to success on their criterion measures. These behaviours were for the most part extrovert in the non-technical sense.

There is an obvious and deep-seated problem in relating behavioural measures of personality traits to learning performance, which concerns the directness of the relationship. Extroversion is a case in point. It may be that an outgoing personality is a valuable asset for a language learner in itself, but this may be confounded in the classroom situation with the equal advantage of a large share of the classroom talk. In other words, extroverts might succeed, if they in fact do, at the expense of introverts because their willingness to talk, to risk failure and to assert themselves is useful to the teacher trying to generate talk opportunities. By the same token, some teachers might regard them as a nuisance and attempt to keep them quiet. So far, studies of this personality trait have not been able to control for this possible interaction of trait and share of classroom attention.

Another personality trait that has received some attention is a person's ability to entertain, more or less patiently, conflicting ideas or hypotheses, at least until such confusion is cleared up by further experience. This is usually referred to as tolerance for ambiguity. In any learning situation it could be a useful characteristic, but in language learning especially so, since it is almost inevitable that explanations or rules will be encountered that apparently conflict with ones given or discovered earlier. Conflict could arise from beliefs about other languages rooted in one's conception of the mother tongue, which would be a special case of the belief congruence dimension cited in the quotation from H. D. Brown on p. 132; or from encountering exceptions to rules that are generally the precursors of a more general and more complex rule. Naiman *et al.* (1975) used Budner's Scale (1962), which is based on the definition of intolerance of ambiguity as a tendency to perceive ambiguous situations as sources of threat and the opposite pole, tolerance, as a tendency to perceive them as desirable. The person checks off a number of descriptions of ambiguous situations as threatening or desirable in various degrees of intensity. Naiman *et al.* found that success on their listening comprehension task, but not on the imitation task, was associated significantly with tolerance as measured by Budner's Scale. Thus we might say that the good listeners in their school sample were not worried by ambiguous situations. Other data they provide show that tolerant students preferred the teacher to use the foreign language more in class and exhibited a lack of ethnocentricity (see below). These results are instructive, but further confirmation is necessary.

Several authors have speculated that the ability to empathise, to take the other person's point of view and be sensitive to others, is a useful characteristic in language learning. Guiora *et al.* (1975) claim to have shown that this characteristic is related to successful language learning, specifically to pronunciation, using a variety of measures such as sensitivity to the significance of facial expressions, projection of empathy in responses to the Thematic Apperception Test (TAT) (see Chapter 10, p. 146) and literary interpretation. The Good Language Learner Project (Naiman *et al.*, 1975) used Hogan's Empathy Scale, but high empathy was not restricted to the group who were successful on the two criterion measures. Empathy was associated, as might be expected, with extroversion and lack of ethnocentricity, and also with a measure of distractibility, the interference test.

Finally in this group of personality characteristics we include ethnocentricity. This variable, a measure of in-group attitudes and orientation to what are believed to be the principles of one's own culture, has consistently been shown to have a small but significant correlation with language learning. The correlation has been negative, which means that language learning is associated with a lack of this trait, or with disagreement with such statements as:

> Foreigners are all right in their place, but they carry it too far when they get too familiar with us.

> It is only natural and right for each person to think that his family is better than any other.
>
> (quoted in Jakobovits, 1970, pp. 266–7)

Such negative correlations were found by Gardner and Lambert (1972) in many of their studies in Canada and elsewhere. Naiman *et al.* also found one with their listening test, also, of course, in Canada. Whether or not this trait is important in other countries and other language learning situations awaits investigation.

The association of particular personality traits and language learning must be regarded as inconclusive at the moment. What research there has been has looked at language students on course; it is possible that personality variables would be more relevant either to the choice of language study in the first place, or to the use of the language once learnt.

Behavioural Strategies

As well as psychometric studies of traits and abilities that correlate with success at learning foreign tongues, there has been some research of a less controlled kind on the sorts of learning strategies and techniques good language learners adopt. Jakobovits (1970) has a twenty-five-item study habits questionnaire (ch. 5.8.11 pp. 278–83) designed to give the teacher information for diagnosis of students' learning problems; unfortunately, this kind of device is very prone to acquiescence, that is, the tendency for the student filling it out to tick off what he thinks is desirable, and to show himself in the best possible light without actually lying.

The Good Language Learner Project (1975) which has already been extensively quoted from in this chapter was conceived to a large extent as an empirical investigation of the observations of Rubin (1975) and Stern (1974) about what successful language learners seem to do.

Many of the dimensions of individual difference mentioned above are subsumed by Stern into strategies. For example, the language knowledge parts of the tests are included in his fourth strategy, 'Technical know-how about how to tackle a language' and some of the personality factors in his third, 'A tolerant and outgoing approach to the target language and empathy with its speakers'. Other strategies, particularly his seventh and eighth, 'Willingness to practise' and 'Willingness to use the language in real communication' refer ultimately to aspects of social behaviour not covered above. In this connection, Pickett (1978) has commented that for his sample of experienced learners the only practice the majority found useful was actual language use, and they did not see the point of making a distinction except to denounce meaningless repetitive practice. Also in this connection, Hatch (1978) has described, on the basis of transcripts of real conversations between native speakers and learners (both adults and children), the kinds of social interaction that in her view characterise such situations, and which all language learners have to survive, consisting of painfully persistent negotiation of topics and repairs of broken-down communication. Some of this work has already been described in Chapter 8. For Hatch, good language learners would be those who learned techniques of keeping the conversation going with echo-responses, requests for rephrasings, supplementary questions, and so on, and she actually advocates teaching such conversational skills in the new language.

Fillmore (1976) has suggested that children, at least, and probably adults also, employ social strategies to obtain and maintain contact in the foreign language in natural situations. The sort of strategies she claims to have identified are the following:

> Join a group and act as if you understand what's going on, even if you don't.

> Give the impression – with a few well-chosen words – that you can speak the language.

> (Fillmore, 1976, p. 5)

Social strategies such as these are obviously personal and idiosyncratic, and can hardly be taught in normal classes. However, where the learning takes place in the country where the language is spoken, strategies such as these can be actively encouraged by activities that send the students out into the community on individual and group project work.

Utility

In the introduction to this chapter, six options for the teacher or other responsible authority were mentioned briefly and discussion of them postponed. Now that some of the better-known parameters of individual difference have been reviewed, it is appropriate to discuss those options. In some cases one is dealing with actual test results such as a teacher finds in a student's file when he or she takes over a group. In these cases the problem of the self-fulfilling prophecy is extremely important, in which the predictions come true not because they were inherently valid but because the teacher's treatment of the students concerned was unwittingly shaped by them. In other cases it may be a question of gaining further information about a student in order to diagnose a learning problem or counsel the student, and a standard test may be used. But in the majority of cases teachers do not have the resources of standardised tests to hand and their knowledge of individual differences is informal and personal; research has taken some of the categories of this knowledge and investigated them in detail, but not comprehensively. The options that teachers have to consider may therefore be seen as strategies for coping with a wide range of kinds of variability among learners.

Ignore differences

The teacher can ignore individual differences, and design and carry out instruction based on knowledge of the language, the educational context and the aims of instruction. Ignoring this kind of knowledge might be seen by some teachers as the only fair thing to do, for two reasons. First, they might argue, all the evidence for relevant individual differences suffers badly from vagueness of definition, confusion with other effects, and problems of causal interpretation (does the correlation between such and such a dimension and language learning reflect that dimension causing the language learning success, or vice versa, or some third unknown factor?). Secondly, they might argue, with considerable justification, that most classrooms contain such a wide variety of learners and therefore aptitudes, styles and personalities, that any modification of materials or technique for particular individual differences is disadvantageous to the majority.

Diagnosis

The teacher can use his knowledge of individual differences to diagnose the reasons for learning problems. Naiman's work on error patterns characteristic of field-independent and -dependent learners has underlined both the diagnostic importance of cognitive style and the general problem which individual differences pose for error analysis. The general problem of student variability was commented on when discussing error analysis in Chapter 8 (p. 110 ff.); in general, the same error might have been produced for several different reasons. Cognitive-style differences may help to disentangle some of these reasons. A student who has overgeneralised a rule to include a number of instances that are really the domain of a different rule may have a general tendency to be a broad categoriser: merely telling that student that overgeneralisation has taken place will not get to the root of the problem, which is to persuade the student to pay more attention to category boundaries in general and, perhaps, to be aware of his or her own tendency to go for an oversimple set of categories. Teachers often attribute learning problems to study habits, or rather, to poor study habits, without there being very much clear evidence of what really constitute good study habits for language learning. Pimsleur's LAB was developed for use as both a selection (see below) and a diagnostic instrument, and he discusses its use for building diagnostic profiles of intending language students in detail in his (1968b) article. With a relatively short test such as the LAB there is the problem that the individual subtests are too short to be reliable on their own, and this inevitably restricts its diagnostic power. In any case, there is a wide gap between diagnosis and treatment; suggestions for effective treatment are more likely to come from the teacher's own sensitivity and experience than from the literature on individual differences.

Student selection

Students can be selected for language study on the basis of tests of relevant individual differences. This was the prime force behind the development of IQ tests in general educational selection and later of aptitude tests for specific subjects. It was justified either by recourse to the argument that the teaching resources were too limited to give every student the possibility of language study, or to the argument that inept students who were likely to fail anyway should be warned against an unsuitable subject and guided towards an area where their personal qualities would flourish. However, in many countries universal public education has adopted, or had forced upon it, a newer interpretation of its responsibilities in which foreign language study is open to all students as of right, and in this situation the selection argument is untenable. It has also become obvious, with the development of newer methods and materials for teaching and with research into increased numbers and kinds of parameters of relevant individual differences, that the older predictive instruments were not accurate enough. For example, the highest correlation claimed by Pimsleur (1968b) was a multiple correlation of + 0·7 between aptitude and general school achievement taken together and achievement in French as a foreign language. Impressive though this sounds, it nevertheless means that there were considerable numbers of students who were successful in the criterion examinations but were not high on either other subject results or aptitude, and vice versa.

Match the method to the student

The competent authority can use the results of individual difference research to design methods of teaching that are matched to the characteristics of the learners. Chastain (1969) raised this question in a slightly different form, asking if it was possible, by statistical hindsight, to work out from the patterns of success and failure on two types of language course, audio-lingual and cognitive-code, and the pattern of responses to a battery of tests of aptitude, modality preference, motivation and abilities, which students would have been better suited to which type of course. He argued that it was possible and that these tests could therefore be used predictively. Although he did not use any learning style measures in that study, the main impetus for the study of learning or cognitive style in the 1960s had been just this possibility of an interaction between personal learning characteristics and particular teaching methods. In general educational theory initial optimism about finding reliable predictions that certain types of students will succeed with certain kinds of method has ebbed, but in language teaching the question of individualisation of instruction is still very much a live issue. It is interesting to note in this connection that H. D. Brown (1977) makes a point of criticising one of the newer methods of teaching, most famous today for its explicit concern with learners as persons with unique things to say, the counselling-learning method (Curran, 1976), precisely on the grounds that the method does not have the flexibility to allow for individual differences in motivation and cognitive style. More traditional approaches to teaching have looked for different ways of catering for individual differences. The opponents of programmed instruction used pace of learning as the principal means of doing this; learners could work through the same programme, but at their own speed. Other variations of the diet of teaching have included the use, or suppression, of explanations, tasks for individual or group completion, students choosing their own reading and writing assignments, and different types of reading exercise, demanding, for instance, a global or a detailed response. (For an up-to-date review of the field of individualisation in language teaching see the Symposium in the *Modern Language Journal*, November 1975.) These variations have usually followed the principle that individualised learning is not the same as isolated learning, but the difference is not always appreciated.

Modify the student

Students may be trained to adopt characteristics that have been shown to be relevant to language learning. It is easier to understand how this option can apply to the strategies discussed by Stern (1974), Rubin (1975) and others, which concern learning tactics, private study habits and social ploys, than how it can apply to more deep-seated qualities such as learning style and aptitude. However, in many cases, training students to be good learners is exactly what teachers have thought education was all about for a very long time. Furthermore the idea that one can teach good study habits for language learning cannot come as a surprise to language teachers, who are professionally involved in teaching study skills for other subjects on an increasing scale. Extending the argument to characteristics of personality and mental ability which are felt to be rather immutable is often considered to be unacceptable. Nevertheless, school exerts tremendous pressure on children and adolescents while their personalities are developing; this pressure may well be the origin of certain cognitive-style and aptitude differences. In discussing field independence the point was made that Naiman *et al.*'s results might theoretically have been the by-product of training by the school system for likely university or college entrance. Here we are considering another possibility, namely, that parents, teachers and schools actually force students to adopt certain habits and abilities which are thought desirable. There is, however, little or no hard evidence on this point. Adults learning outside the school system, individually or in specialist language schools, are obviously not subject to these strong and often hidden pressures to the same degree.

Match students and teachers

Students with certain personal characteristics may be matched with teachers who also have those characteristics. In general educational psychology this option has been treated as the problem of matching learning style with teaching style. Thelen's work (1967) quoted in Chapter 7 confirmed the suspicion that not every teacher was equally good with every kind of learner, but queried whether match or mismatch of style was desirable. In research into language instruction there has been no study of this question, and yet it is a matter of common experience that teachers who are equally imaginative and equally conscientious are not necessarily equally successful with every kind of learner. Many customers for EFL courses differ considerably in what they expect teachers to do and how they expect them to behave, because their own cultures have different interpretations of the nature of education and the role of the teacher and what kinds of study methods are appropriate and acceptable. Although the arguments for matching teaching and learning styles are not conclusive, teachers who are not at least aware of and sensitive to these personal and cultural differences may encounter unexpected problems.

Summary

This chapter has reviewed some of the better-known dimensions of individual differences in learning which may be relevant for language learning, and considered the options open to teachers, administrators and materials writers in catering for them. It seems essential for practitioners in the field to be aware of their students as individuals and to be sensitive to the many kinds of differences which may exist even in one learning group. Which of the options for coping with this situation will be chosen is a question that can only be answered by the professional teacher in possession of all the facts about the objectives of the course, the resources of the teaching situation, the students themselves and their language needs. For more extensive treatments of this issue the reader is referred to the articles by Cohen (1977) and Hosenfeld (1976).

Chapter 10

Motivation

Let us say that, *given motivation*, it is inevitable that a human being will learn a second language if he is exposed to the language data. (Corder, 1967, p. 164)

Most language teachers will agree that the motivation of the students is one of the most important factors influencing their success or failure in learning the language. Indeed this is a truism equally applicable to any other school subject. Teachers may disagree, however, in their estimates of the proportion which is contributed by the students themselves and the proportion which is contributed by the teacher's own actions and the activities making up the language instruction. Just as motivation is certainly important for any learning operation, so it is important to attempt to find out some acceptable answer to the question of relative contributions, because the designers of future language instruction (both materials writers and trainers of teachers) need to know what aspects of motivation are amenable to manipulation and when and where and how.

Naturally the sociological factors affecting language learning situations which Schumann refers to as creating social distance play an important role here (see Chapter 6). The language teacher who finds himself caught between possibly hostile cultures, or cast as the representative of a resented or resisted culture, has immense problems in coping with these intangible pressures. In what follows, attention is directed more to the motives that appear to play an immediate role in the learning process, than to the socio-cultural background, although the distinction is difficult to draw precisely.

There are, however, some dangers inherent in the blanket term 'motivation'. For example, some inexperienced teachers may confuse the generating of enthusiasm, undoubtedly an important motivational element, with the whole task of motivating the students to undertake and persevere with work. There is also the danger, in assessing motivation on the basis of questionnaires and interviews, of expecting actual behaviour to be entirely predictable from expressed attitudes. These are perhaps marginal and uncommon dangers; more serious is the tendency to use the term 'motivation' as a general cover term – a dustbin – to include a number of possibly distinct concepts, each of which may have different origins and different effects and require different classroom treatment. There is thus an obvious pedagogic problem. There is also a problem of extrapolation, because the findings in the psychology of motivation will often be difficult to extrapolate justifiably to the pedagogic situation, unless the resemblance of the experimental situation to the teaching one is very close.

For example, one should distinguish at least between

(a) energy
(b) willingness to learn
(c) perseverance
(d) interest
(e) enjoyment of lessons
(f) incentives
(g) benefits of knowing the language.

Many, more detailed, distinctions could be drawn. The origin of any of these variables for any particular learner may well be different from that of other learners. The classroom treatment they can be given also differs. Willingness to learn may be related to parental encouragement (not necessarily positively), or to happy learning experiences in other subjects, or to some temperamental trait. Interest may be original to the student, or it may have come via a parent, another relative, another student, a visit, or a television show. Interest is often regarded as being a major element in the teacher's store of motivational tactics: if the pupil's interest is aroused perseverance, and so on, may be increased. Rewards, incentives, variety of classroom activity are further tactics available to the teacher, but their effects on success will depend on their quality, and on the pupils' own scale of values, which in turn may have been partly formed by the effectiveness of other motivational tactics – in a sense, by the success of the teacher's advertising of the benefits of learning! The complications arising in discussions of motivation are thus evident:

(1) The word generally refers to a collection of possibly distinct concepts.
(2) The sources of motivation may or may not be present in the classroom.
(3) Only a few types of motivation are under the instructor's control.
(4) Some types seem to be more closely related to the product of learning (qualifications, proficiency); others to the process (success or incentives for particular tasks, choice of language variety).
(5) The effectiveness of any technique is determined by the students' own scale of values.

Psychological Views of Motivation

Drive

The study of motivation was long dominated by the concept of drive. For psychologists such as Hull and Thorndike (see Weiner, 1972a) this was energy directed toward a given goal. This energy was considered to arise from the difference between the body's actual internal state and a state of physical equilibrium or 'homeostasis'. The major homeostatic needs of mammals are air, water, food and constant body temperature. Thus, in ordinary language, a man is driven to eat because his body needs food. By extension, he might be driven to learn because learning gives him rewards — approval, tokens of success — which have been associated in the past with the satisfaction of homeostatic needs. In animal experiments on learning, the reward given to the animal for successful learning, and the reinforcement given during behaviour shaping, was often food, and thus satisfied a primary need. Thus the animal had drive to learn because the learning was rewarded by satisfaction of the primary need. In most animal learning experiments, the primary need — hunger — had to be induced first, by withholding food. There have been many developments and elaborations on this basic homeostatic drive theory, but there are two crucial reasons why it has to be rejected for serious consideration in connection with human learning.

The first is that drive to act (in this case, to learn) is reduced if the need is reduced: therefore giving reward reduces learning instead of increasing it. Thus an animal trainer has to regulate his rewards so that the animal retains drive (because it remains hungry) to the end of the training. It is clear, however, that this kind of drive theory is not particularly useful in analysing complex human learning problems because need reduction does not necessarily take place. Although human learners often have well-defined aims and objectives, the satisfaction of homeostatic needs is irrelevant to them. For example, learning part of a language may increase motivational strength: that is, the learner may want to learn the rest. Also, although learning the language is pursued with a particular goal in view, the satisfaction or payoff from the activity of learning itself may be just as great as that from the final attainment of the goal. Simple conceptions of drive theory confuse these aspects of motivation.

The second reason to reject the needs-based drive theory is its mechanistic nature. Drive was held to result automatically from the development of a need, without reference to any more sophisticated set of values. In humans, the effect of any reward of knowledge of results is dependent on values and perceptions rather than mechanistic reactions, and this will be discussed in more detail below. More modern conceptions of drive have disassociated it from biological needs. Drive is defined as what makes us act, which avoids the above problems but is very vague.

Expectancy and Value

An area of research to which a great deal of attention was directed in the late 1930s and the 1940s was that concerned with how difficult a task a person would elect to perform after having some experience of success or failure in similar tasks. This was called the 'level of aspiration'. Much very valuable information was gathered in the quite simple experimental situation which this research used, which consisted generally of having subjects choose tasks, perform them, and then choose another from a selection which differed in difficulty. In general, previous success raises the level of aspiration; previous failure lowers it. However, the level of aspiration may be affected by many subtle factors. For example, ease of task, nature of task, value placed on task, expectations of performance, comparisons with other groups and anxiety may all affect the level. A very easily gained success is followed by a low setting of aspiration; a closed task such as problem-solving produces more consistent levels of aspiration than a task which appears to have a large element of luck; a task which is highly valued may produce a lower level of aspiration (because the pain of failure will be greater) than a low-valued task; the way others (especially teachers) expect a person to perform affects the way that person expects to perform; an anxious person may set a low level to avoid failure, or may set a high level which is possibly unrealistic, perhaps because failure can be explained away because the task was too difficult anyway. The many absorbing results of work in this area are summarised by Vernon (1969).

The theoretical basis of this approach was Kurt Lewin's 'Field Theory', the relevant part of which stated that the level of aspiration would be determined by the interaction of two main factors: the person's estimate of his likelihood of succeeding on the task and the importance to him of success on the task, which Lewin termed its 'valence'. This was clearly a different kind of theory to those discussed above under the general heading of the concept of drive, and the difference is exactly in the willingness to attribute differences in behaviour to internal, subjective factors. Moreover, this type of description of behaviour directed toward some goal did not require the suggestion of a return to some balanced state of homeostatic satisfaction, as the need reduction theory of drive had done. In Lewin's theory, motivation depended on two evaluations, valence and chances of success, and they were not always independent. Sometimes the valence of a task might depend on whether you think you can do it or not.

However, the work on level of aspiration provided results that can be directly useful in the classroom, for example, if the teacher is persuading pupils to opt for work assignments of differing difficulty. The teacher's problem in such a case is to persuade the pupil not so much that a given level of difficulty is suitable, for that will be apparent to the pupil from (a) his/her experience with similar problems, and (b) how many of his/her class mates he/she knows have succeeded, but that it is worth his/her effort in terms of the pupil's own values. As will be seen later, this point may be a difficult one, depending among other things on sex, age, parental encouragement, class size and the headmaster's attitude!

Nevertheless, level of aspiration is a crucial variable in any learning situation. Many school pupils have low levels of aspiration and the reasons are not usually hard to see. Some are enshrined in the institutional structure, with ability groupings that carry an unmistakable and depressing message to those in the lower ability groups. Others are communicated by subtle social pressures from peers, parents and social milieu.

Need for achievement (nAch)

The learner's estimates of the value of the task to him (either in the long term or the short term), and the chances of succeeding, are clearly vital components of the motivation. However, there are further complications. One very important set of individual differences has been studied under the heading 'need for achievement', often shortened to nAch. The word 'need' here does not imply a basic bodily need.

The strength of nAch was considered by Atkinson (1957) to be the net result of two tendencies, motivation toward success and motivation toward avoidance of failure. One of the implications of this conception is that individuals may have the same net nAch, but they could be of different character, that is, different mixtures of drive to go and get success or to avoid failure. Their actual performance might well be different. The origins of these two aspects of nAch could be in different experiences in early childhood, and parental attitudes. Both of these tendencies were conceived of as being composed of three factors:

(1)   the person's expectations of success (or failure)
(2)   the value of the task as an incentive
(3)   the orientation toward success or toward avoidance of failure.

The first two components are assessable by the level of aspiration technique as in Lewin's theory. The third component can be assessed by interview or by the projective technique invented by H. A. Murray, the Thematic Apperception Test (TAT). In this, a set of carefully ambiguous pictures are shown and the person is invited to create stories around each. It is assumed that the person's own feelings will be projected into the stories and therefore they are examined for the proportion of references to success, striving, failure, inadequacy and so forth.

This theory and its subsequent elaborations have been shown in much experimentation to be a very powerful tool for predicting and understanding achievement-related behaviour. A large amount of that research has been in educational contexts, though not directly in second language classrooms. For example, one implication of the theory, reported by Weiner (1972) is that programmed instruction of the Skinnerian type is more effective for pupils in whom avoidance of failure is stronger than striving for success, whereas pupils who have high success orientation will become bored because the chances of success on each frame are practically certain. In less theoretical language, these latter pupils need more of a challenge. Another implication (Atkinson and O'Connor, 1963, reported in Weiner, p. 233) is that division of students into homogeneous or heterogeneous groups (that is, streamed or mixed ability groups) may be more or less effective according to the type of motivation of a particular student. Students dominated by striving for success may thrive in homogeneous groups; those dominated by avoidance of failure may thrive in mixed ability groups. The evidence that this is true is, however, ambiguous.

Before going on to look at one further modern approach to motivation, attribution theory, there is one important respect in which generalisations on the basis of achievement theory are inadequate. Put crudely, it works for men but not for women. This may be because men and women differ in their reactions to projective techniques such as the TAT, or because a woman's motivation for success may (still) be more likely to bring her into conflict with the role expected of her by society, than a man's. In the educational context, it has even been suggested that high-achieving girls develop a will to fail during their last years at school, in response to social pressures (Maccoby and Jacklin, 1973, quoted by Burstall, 1975). But in language classes, more specifically French, Burstall's (1975) report of the evaluation of the Primary French Project in Britain shows that this is not so: the attitudes of the adolescent girls towards their French lessons and their achievement in French remained consistently more favourable and higher, respectively, than those of the boys. This is presumably because learning a language does not conflict with society's norms for educated girls, whereas achievement in mathematics or engineering might. Measures of these girls' achievement needs were not taken; a direct study of achievement needs, sex and language learning is still wanted.

Attribution theory

The last theoretical position on motivation to be briefly reviewed here is the most cognitive and non-mechanistic yet to appear. Attribution theory attempts to describe motivated behaviour in terms of the cause to which the individuals attribute, or ascribe, their own and other people's performance: their own ability, effort, intention, or others' ability, effort, or intention, luck, and so on. In so doing, it represents an attempt to elaborate the three-component theory just outlined and include perceptions, motives and ideas which learners think influence their own performance – which may loosely be called 'cognitions'.

As an example of the kind of reasoning involved, Weiner (1972b) points out that one would not necessarily go to a film simply on someone else's recommendation, but the decision would depend on whether you attributed the recommendation to the fact that the film was good or to the fact that the person was easily pleased. In the educational context he and his co-workers have shown that the principle that attribution of responsibility guides subsequent behaviour is true of both teachers and pupils. For example, Weiner and Kukla (1970, reviewed by Weiner, 1972b) have demonstrated that trainee teachers give praise and punishment according to whether they perceive a pupil's score to be the result of ability or the lack of it, or effort or the lack of it. Pupils who were thought to be dull but hard-working were given more praise than pupils perceived to be of high ability and hard-working whose results were otherwise equivalent. Pupils perceived to be dull and lazy were praised more often than bright but lazy pupils. Thus, effort to overcome a handicap was highly valued by these student teachers; encouragement was especially given where an increase in effort was seen as a possible remedy, but failing to work hard enough to fulfil one's potential was punished. Although this experiment did not use experienced teachers and did not take place in the classroom, replications with experienced teachers have been reported. In the classroom, Brophy and Good (1974, p. 98) have conducted a study in which pupils believed to be of high ability were praised more often for correct answers, criticised less for incorrect ones and given more help to answer questions than pupils believed to be of low ability. (Their study did not look at the perceived effort variable.)

Students and pupils also differ in their attitudes to their own work in terms of responsibility (their own or others'), ability and effort. Weiner quotes a study by Cook of children learning a series of puzzles. Each time a child experienced success or failure he took or gave back a number of reward tokens to indicate how much he thought he deserved. Broadly, a child gives himself greatest reward when he thinks success is due to great effort – he then feels most proud – and punishes himself most when he thinks he hasn't worked hard enough. These cognitions are formed by the learner and, of course, may easily disagree with the teacher's cognition of the causes of the pupil's success or failure. Weiner (1972b) draws further and most interesting implications from attribution theory. For example, these causal attributions are also linked to achievement striving; thus a pupil's feeling of pride in accomplishment or shame in failure is not only linked backwards to the causes he perceives, but also forwards to how hard he will strive at the next task, or learning problem. For example, individuals who have high need for achievement tend to ascribe success to personal factors – their own ability and hard work. People who take personal credit for success feel greater pride in achievement than people who attribute their success to outside factors; this augmented pride tends to lead to more attempts to achieve things – to climb to greater heights. Similarly individuals who have high need for achievement tend to ascribe failure to not working hard enough. Effort is relatively unstable; it can be varied more or less at will. Therefore failure is seen by these individuals as a temporary setback; later successes can be anticipated. However, individuals who are not very ambitious tend to ascribe failure to lack of ability, which is not directly under their control, and therefore failure is likely to mean to them a vision of continuing failure. Thus individual differences in willingness to learn and perseverance are linked to achievement needs and in turn to attributional tendencies. In the case of language learners, one of the most frequent attributions to a stable factor outside their control is to aptitudes such as an ear for languages. Thus a language learner may easily save face by ascribing failure to a physical disposition: 'I'm no mug but I've got no ear for languages'.

This type of theory highlights the extreme complexity of motivation; apart from the difficulty of finding out where the individual differences come from, presumably in part from parents, school atmosphere, teachers, and so on, there is the added problem of conflict of opinion between pupil and teacher. A not very ambitious pupil may think 'I failed because I'm a mug' whereas the teacher may argue that failure was due to lack of effort. Also, the estimation of how difficult a task is going to be will depend partly on how similar it is expected to be to previous tasks and how the student fared at them, and also whether the student has any information about how many other students passed or failed at the task. One quite stable result in the literature of attribution theory has been that individuals who have high need for achievement tend to go for tasks where they think there is a roughly equal chance of success or failure, whereas others go either for easy tasks because they virtually guarantee success, or for difficult tasks because failure can be attributed to outside factors, namely, the difficulty. If, of course, they have no obvious way of assessing the difficulty, either by reference to their own experience or to that of other students, they will tend to think 'I'm a mug'.

Motivation of Language Learners

So far, we have concentrated on general psychological views of motivated behaviour in educational contexts, but very little of this work has been directly concerned with language classes. There are, however, special problems in language learning. Achievement in language learning is many-sided: some students wish to become linguists, translators, interpreters, and so forth; others to get prestigious jobs; others to survive on other courses taught in the new language (perhaps in competition with native speakers); others, in some parts of the world, to identify with the other language community. Yet others, like learners of foreign languages at school in Britain, have goals set for them by the education system but may not personally experience any benefit from learning the language until after leaving school, if then. Moreover, the relationship between interest in a language and its speakers and achievement in it is complex, and here the instructor has an important role to play as a manager of cultural contact. But, as in most other fields, the incentive value of success is the most important variable. In this connection the instructor, his handling of the materials and his treatment of individual students' success or failure play an all-important role in engineering continuing success: and we have already seen how complex the effects of success on different individuals can be. But success is not simply a matter of being told 'That's right'. Success automatically brings certain benefits, or rewards, in terms of the material learnt.

Strength

Stevick (1971) has suggested that there are at least five types of reward available to an instructor or to a materials writer or adapter, in language teaching materials and classes. He classes them together under his concept of 'strength'. By strength he means a criterion illustrated by this question: 'Does [the material] carry its own weight by means of the rewards that it makes available?' The five types of reward may be glossed as:

(1) Relevance – of the content to the student's own language needs.
(2) Completeness – inclusion of all the language necessary for the stated aims of the course.
(3) Authenticity – the material should be both linguistically and culturally authentic.
(4) Satisfaction – the student should leave each lesson feeling he has benefited more than simply progressed.
(5) Immediacy – the student can use the material in a lesson straight away.

(1), (2) and (3) apply to whole courses, (4) and (5) more particularly to individual lessons. One would not expect to find all these aspects of strength present in any one piece of teaching material, indeed it may not be desirable. Oversell can be self-defeating. But none of these features have any strength unless they are perceived by the consumer – the learner – to be reliable. Stevick makes the important point that value within the classroom is related to the ease with which a situation requiring a particular language form can be created, but that is not in turn related to the frequency with which a similar situation occurs in real life. If the students are expected to perceive a link with life outside the classroom, then the material or classroom activity must have strength in this sense – relevance.

Stevick's definition of strength introduces the concept of 'weight': the rewards are motivational devices which balance off the weight, or difficulty, proportion of new material, length of unit, of the material to be learnt. We have already seen how the perceived difficulty of a task varies with the learner's past history, which in this case is (a) his previous success in the language, (b) his understanding of prior material necessary for the new point and (c) his first language, and with his estimate of how many others will succeed, if it is group instruction. Strength and weight are therefore interdependent, and can only be estimated by reference to the actual student's cognitions of value.

Orientation to the language

Cognitions of value may be affected by another variable which has received considerable attention in bilingual situations such as Montreal. Gardner and Lambert (1972) have performed a long series of correlational studies measuring the extent to which achievement in the second language is related either to a desire to use the language in the context of the student's own community, for business, or promotion, or simply to possess a prestigious qualification; or to a desire to become accepted by, or even become a member of, the community that speaks the other language. These two different reasons for study have been labelled respectively 'instrumental' and 'integrative' orientations to language learning. They have found that in places like Montreal, where English- and French-speaking Canadians live side by side, higher achievement in the other language is usually associated with the integrative orientation.

The definitions of these two types of orientation have never been particularly precise and have undergone some changes over the twenty years of research by Gardner and Lambert. However, the important factor is the way these motives are expressed in the questions asked of the learners, since their strength is inferred from the answers. An instrumental orientation is diagnosed from agreement with the following statements:

The study of [French] can be important to me because:
(1) I need it to finish high school
(2) One needs a good knowledge of at least one foreign language to merit social recognition
(3) I think it will some day be useful in getting a good job
(4) I feel that no one is really educated unless he is fluent in [French].
                                        (adapted from Jakobovits, 1970, pp. 270–1)

These statements all refer to indications of success of various kinds within the learner's own community; although no correlational study with more traditional measures of nAch has been carried out, it seems very likely that people agreeing strongly with these statements would also exhibit high achievement motivation. An integrative orientation to language learning is diagnosed from agreement with the following statements:

The study of [French] can be important to me because:
(5) It will enable me to gain good friends more easily among [French]-speaking people
(6) It will help me understand better the [French]-speaking people and way of life
(7) It will allow me to meet and converse with more and varied people

(8)   It should enable me to think and behave as do the [French]-speaking people.

(adapted from Jakobovits, 1970, pp. 270–1)

These statements illustrate two aspects of integrative motivation which should perhaps be kept separate. On the one hand, there is a general desire for wider social contact in (5), (6) and (7) among speakers of the language in the same city (the research was originally conducted in bilingual Montreal). This motive seems to be a special case of a social pressure for affiliation. This affiliative motive is a very important aspect of human motivation in general, and it has been studied in various contexts, including the development of various social skills aimed at maximising social contact (Argyle, 1967). On the other hand, statement (8) contains a much stronger belief, that learning the language will in some sense let the individual acquire the psychological characteristics of the other group, or take on a persona similar to that attributed to the other group. This is a much stronger claim. It is more than affiliation, it is belonging. In several of Gardner and Lambert's studies that show a positive correlation between integrative orientation and achievement it is not clear whether the students were motivated by the affiliative tendency or the belief that they could become members of the other community. In one study of Spolsky's (1969), foreigners learning English for study in the USA did appear to be integratively motivated in the latter sense. The most successful learners of English were those who wanted to assume personality characteristics they thought typical of Americans rather than of their own cultures. Spolsky's study used a different method, a checklist of adjectives describing personality traits which the learners rated for their relevance to themselves and how they would like to be, and for the home and the new cultures.

However, it is rather unlikely that the second, stronger sense of the integrative motive is effective for many learners. In Canada, Gardner and Smythe (1975) still find that an integrative motive is dominant among many learners in Toronto, and point to both achievement figures and drop-out rate (lower for integratively motivated than instrumentally motivated learners). Their use of the term integrative, however, covers both integration and affiliation and also general attitudes, including those towards the language classes and to French Canadians, and therefore is even weaker than the earlier version. In other countries instrumental motivation has been found to be more powerful, for example, in the Philippines (Gardner and Lambert, 1972, pp. 121–30) and Bombay (Lukmani, 1972).

There is a basic difficulty with all these studies which makes causal inference impossible. The questionnaires and tests have usually been administered to learners who are on course, that is to say, in the middle of courses of instruction. Therefore a finding that eventual success of teacher's ratings of progress is related to agreement with this or that set of statements or this or that motivational tendency cannot be held to mean that success is because of the particular attitudes discovered any more than that the attitudes are the result of successful progress. In fact, it is quite likely that most if not all of the orientations to the learning experience reported could have been the result and not the cause of successful progress. If someone is enjoying a course, for whatever reason, this might well encourage positive attitudes to eventual payoff in terms of job prospects, social recognition, affiliation and even integrating in certain special circumstances.

Attitudes

It seems unlikely that achievement in foreign languages in British and European schools is affected by integrative motives. Two recent research projects in Britain have investigated the relationship between attitudes and achievement in foreign languages. Boys' attitudes to German in a grammar school were investigated in the course of Green's (1975) study of language laboratory use at York. For these boys, liking German was not dependent on whether they had favourable opinions of the people or country – but, as the researchers point out, they had direct experience only of the language. Moreover, there was only a weak relationship between achievement and attitudes towards the language and no relationship between achievement and attitudes towards the people or country. It may well be that these pupils regarded German as (just) another school subject rather than something special which was a live language. In psychological terms, then, it would be reasonable to predict that material which stressed the utility of German for, for example, making German friends, or understanding German culture would not have been very successful for these pupils. There is no way of assessing how widespread this configuration of attitudes is.

In the final summing-up of the ten-year evaluation of the Primary French in Britain scheme Burstall (1975) reports that through both primary and secondary school attitudes to learning French are strongly related to success in the language. Their measure of attitudes was a medium-length questionnaire containing items referring to the country, the people, ease of learning, comparisons with other subjects, utility for jobs, and so on (see Burstall, 1975, Appendix, p. 247). However, in discussing an association between attitudes or orientations to learning, and achievement, it is only possible to make causal inferences, that is, state which affected which, in a longitudinal study. Furthermore, the evaluation of primary French by the National Foundation for Educational Research (NFER) studied three year-groups of pupils from primary school to school-leaving and compared attitude and achievement scores at all stages. This indicated that early success was more frequently associated with favourable attitudes at later stages, and with success at later stages, than early favourable attitudes were with later attitudes or achievement. Burstall comments: 'In the language learning situation, nothing succeeds like success.'

It also became clear that integrative attitudes decreased in favour of instrumental attitudes after age 11 or 12 and markedly in secondary school; this may be related to the growing maturity of the pupils and their increasing concern with employment prospects, but also to the fact that integrative attitudes to French people – wanting to converse, make friends, were shared by many who did not like learning the language, and subsequently left the classes. If the latter explanation is true, it contrasts with the situation in Toronto referred to in the previous section about the observations of Gardner and Smythe. There was also a marked difference between the sexes. Girls' attitudes to learning French were consistently more favourable than boys' – which is perhaps not surprising, given the social pressures via parents, the media and prospective employers. This difference does not appear to be related to an integrative orientation. Visits to France and contact with French speakers were significantly related to both higher achievement (but there is a socio-economic variable here – offspring of richer parents in richer areas tend to achieve more anyway, and these are the ones that go on the visits) and more favourable attitudes in both boys and girls. They were a powerful incentive, but more often in an instrumental sense than an integrative one.

Conclusion

The review of psychological analyses of motivation presented here with a summary of some of the recent research in second language learning relevant to motivation has shown that the ways in which a student is motivated to choose to do some learning, or to learn willingly if he has no choice, and to persevere with the learning, are varied and complex. The role of the teacher is equally delicate. The effects of success on a learning task are not simple. The effects of failure may be equally complex. Both differ between individuals according to their achievement needs, characteristic attributional tendencies, perceived position in relation to other members of the group, ideas about the value to them of learning the language, and the ways the teacher normally treats them. Language teachers need to be aware of these problems and the results of investigations into them in order to plan and manage instruction that will be optimally efficient for each student, at least to the extent that it is within their power at all to influence the students' choice and perseverance.

Epilogue

In the preceding chapters I have attempted to show how psychological knowledge informs language teaching, in particular in the areas of learning processes, social interaction, psycholinguistics, language development and individual differences. If I had to sum up the role of psychology in language teaching in a few words, they would be understanding, evaluation and suggestion.

As language teachers, we need to understand as much as possible about the language teaching/language learning process. The point has already been made that although individuals are, ultimately, unpredictable in detail, there are broad trends and general categories which can be known and prepared for. Understanding the language learning process involves understanding general principles of learning, principles of the nature of human communication via language, principles of social interaction, in general and in the classroom, and principles of second language development.

Techniques, activities, situations and methods of teaching have to be evaluated for inclusion in a language teaching programme. As we have seen, the relationship between a teaching technique and the theoretical principles on which it is based is often indirect and complex, but if those theoretical principles are challenged by research (a remarkably common fate for theoretical principles, and one which tends to confuse many teachers who are interested in the bases of their profession), other justifications for the technique have to be relied on, and if those justifications are also unsound, alternative techniques have to be sought. One of the tasks of psychology in relation to any teaching application is to research the justification, effectiveness, and limitations of teaching techniques. An example where this has happened over a period of years is the pattern drill technique invented by the early audio-lingualists, discussed at the end of Chapter 2.

Suggestions for new ways of teaching may also arise from psychology. Perhaps the most obvious example of this is the emergence in the last twenty years of the so-called Counselling-Learning technique (Curran, 1976), which attempts to cast the teacher in the role of a non-directive clinical therapist. However, less dramatic and less controversial examples can be found, such as the proposals for exercises encouraging prediction, anticipation and questioning strategies in reading and listening.

In the introductory chapter a more formal approach to these aspects of the role of psychology was adopted. There, five kinds of analysis were proposed as a framework for the proper use of psychological information in designing language teaching courses and teaching methodologies. They were:

(1)   analysis of the conditions that can be manipulated to change a novice into an expert
(2)   analysis of competent performance
(3)   analysis of the development of competent performance
(4)   analysis of the initial state of the learner
(5)   evaluation of the process and the product of learning.

This book has attempted to provide teachers, and others interested in and responsible for language teaching (in particular, English language teaching) with examples of those analyses, drawn from various kinds of language teaching, and the psychological information relevant in each case. However, the book will have failed if it does not provide sufficient information and examples to enable the reader to analyse and evaluate his or her own teaching situation and teaching style with profit and hope for improvement.

Bibliography

Aitchison, J. (1976), *The Articulate Mammal* (London: Hutchinson).

Allwright, R. (1975), 'Problems in the study of teacher's treatment of error', in M. Burt and H. Dulay (eds), *On TESOL '75* (Washington, DC: TESOL).

Annett, J. (1969), *Feedback and Human Behaviour* (Harmondsworth: Penguin).

Argyle, M. (1967), *The Psychology of Interpersonal Behaviour* (Harmondsworth: Penguin).

Atkinson, J. W. (1957), 'Motivational determinants of risk-taking behaviour', *Psychological Review*, vol. 64, pp. 59–72.

Bailey, M., Madden, C., and Krashen, S. D. (1974), 'Is there a "natural sequence" in adult second language learning?', *Language Learning*, vol. 24, no. 2, pp. 235–43.

Bartlett, F. (1932), *Remembering* (Cambridge: CUP).

Bellack, A. A., Kliebard, H. M., Hyman, R. T., and Smith, F. L. Jr (1966), *The Language of the Classroom* (New York: Teachers College Press).

Berko, J. (1958), 'The child's learning of English morphology', *Word*, vol. 14, pp. 150–77.

Berlin, B., and Kay, P. (1969), *Basic Colour Terms: Their Universality and Evolution* (Berkeley, Calif.: University of California Press).

Bever, T. G. (1970), 'The cognitive basis for linguistic structures', in J. R. Hayes (ed.), *Cognition and the Development of Language* (New York: Wiley).

Billows, F. L. (1961), *The Techniques of Language Learning* (London: Longman).

Bloomfield, L. (1933), *Language* (New York: Holt, Rinehart & Winston).

Bousfield, W. A. (1953), 'The occurrence of clustering in the recall of randomly arranged associates', *Journal of General Psychology*, vol. 49, pp. 229–40.

Bower, G. (1976), 'Experiments on story understanding and recall', *Quarterly Journal of Experimental Psychology*, vol. 28, pp. 511–34.

Bracht, G. H., and Glass, G. U. (1972), 'Interaction of personological variables and treatment', in Sperry (1972), ch. 8.

Bransford, J. D., and Johnson, M. K. (1972), 'Conceptual prerequisites for understanding: some investigations of comprehension and recall', *Journal of Verbal Learning and Verbal Behaviour*, vol. 11, pp. 717–26.

Broadbent, D. (1961), *Behaviour* (London: Methuen).

Brophy, J., and Good, T. (1974), *Teacher–Student Relationships. Causes and Consequences* (New York: Holt, Rinehart & Winston).

Broughton, G. (ed.) (1968), *Success with English* (Harmondsworth: Penguin).

Brown, H. D. (1973), 'Affective variables in second language acquisition', *Language Learning*, vol. 23, pp. 231–44.

Brown, H. D. (1977), 'Some limitations of C–L/CLL models of second language teaching', *TESOL Quarterly*, vol. 11, pp. 365–72.

Brown, R. (1973), *A First Language: The Early Stages* (Harmondsworth: Penguin).

Bruner, J. (1975), 'The ontogenesis of speech acts', *Journal of Child Language*, vol. 2, pp. 1–19.

Bruner, J., Goodnow, J., and Austin, G. (1956), *A Study of Thinking* (New York: Wiley).

Bryan, W. L., and Harter, N. (1899), 'Studies on the telegraphic language. The acquisition of a hierarchy of habits', *Psychological Review*, vol. 6, pp. 345–75.

Burstall, C. (1975), *Primary French in the Balance* (Windsor: National Foundation for Educational Research).

Cancino, H., Rosansky, E., and Schumann, J. H. (1978), 'The acquisition of English negatives and interrogatives by native Spanish speakers', in E. M. Hatch (ed.), *Second Language Acquisition* (Rowley, Mass.: Newbury House), pp. 207–30.

Carroll, J. B. (1966), 'The contributions of psychological theory and educational research to the teaching of foreign languages', in A. Valdman (ed.), *Trends in Language Teaching* (New York: McGraw-Hill).

Carroll, J. B. (1971), 'Current issues in psycholinguistics and second language teaching', *TESOL Quarterly*, vol. 5, pp. 101–14.

Carroll, J. B., and Sapon, S. (1959), *Modern Language Aptitude Test* (New York: Psychological Corporation).

Chastain, K. (1969), 'Prediction of success in audio-lingual and cognitive classes', *Language Learning*, vol. 19, pp. 27–39.

Chastain, K. (1971), *The Development of Modern Language Skills: Theory to Practice* (Philadelphia, Pa: Center for Curriculum Development).

Chaudron, C. (1977), 'A descriptive model of discourse in the corrective treatment of learners' errors', *Language Learning*, vol. 27, no. 1, pp. 29–46.

Chomsky, C. S. (1969), *The Acquisition of Syntax from Five to Ten* (Cambridge, Mass.: MIT Press).

Chomsky, N. (1957), *Syntactic Structures* (The Hague: Mouton).

Chomsky, N. (1959), review of Skinner (1957) in *Language*, vol. 35, pp. 26–58.

Chomsky, N. (1965), *Aspects of the Theory of Syntax* (Cambridge, Mass.: MIT Press).

Clark, E. (1973), 'What's in a word? On the child's acquisition of semantics in his first language', in T. Moore (ed.), *Cognitive Development and the Acquisition of Language* (New York: Academic Press).

Clark, H., and Clark, E. (1977), *Psychology and Language* (New York: Harcourt Brace Jovanovich).

Clark, R. (1974), 'Performing without competence', *Journal of Child Language*, vol. 1, pp. 1–10.

Cohen, A. (1977), 'Successful second language speakers: a review of research literature', *Balshaunt Shimushit, Journal of the Israeli Association for Applied Linguistics*, vol. 1, pp. 3–22.

Cook, V. J. (1973), 'Comparison of language development in native children and foreign adults', *International Review of Applied Linguistics*, vol. 11, no. 1, pp. 13–28.

Cook, V. J. (1977), 'Cognitive processes in second language acquisition', *International Review of Applied Linguistics*, vol. 15, pp. 1–20.

Corder, S. P. (1967), 'The significance of learners' errors', *International Review of Applied Linguistics*, vol. 5, pt 4, pp. 161–70; reprinted in J. C. Richards, *Error Analysis* (London: Longman, 1974), pp. 19–27.

Corder, S. P. (1974), *Introducing Applied Linguistics* (Harmondsworth: Penguin).

Cromer, R. F. (1970), 'Children are nice to understand: surface structure due for the recovery of deep structure', *British Journal of Psychology*, vol. 61, pp. 397–408.

Curran, C. A. (1976), *Counseling–Learning in Second Languages* (Apple River, Ill.: Apple River Press).

Dakin, J. (1973), *The Language Laboratory and Language Learning* (London: Longman).

D'Anglejan, A., and Tucker, G. R. (1975), 'The acquisition of complex English structures by adult learners', *Language Learning*, vol. 25, no. 2, pp. 281–96.

Davis, J. H. (1969), *Group Performance* (Reading, Mass.: Addison-Wesley).

Derwing, B. (1973), *Transformational Grammar as a Theory of Language Acquisition* (Cambridge: CUP).

Deutsch, J. A. (1956), 'The inadequacy of the Mullian derivations of reasoning and latent learning', *Psychological Review*, vol. 63, pp. 389–99.

Dinneen, F. P. (1967), *Introduction to General Linguistics* (New York: Holt, Rinehart & Winston).

Donaldson, M., and Balfour, G. (1968), 'Less is more: a study of language comprehension in children', *British Journal of Psychology*, vol. 59, pp. 461–72.

Dulay, H., and Burt, M. (1974), 'A new perspective on the creative construction process in child second language acquisition', *Language Learning*, vol. 24, no. 2, pp. 254–77.

Ebbinghaus, H. (1885), *Über das Gedächtnis* (Leipzig: Duncker); trans. H. Ruger and C. E. Busenius, Teachers College, Columbia University, 1913.

Eilers, R. E., Oller, D. K., and Ellington, J. (1974), 'The acquisition of word meaning for dimensional adjectives: the long and the short of it', *Journal of Child Language*, vol. 1, pp. 195–204.

Ervin, S. (1964), 'Imitation and structural change in children's language', in E. H. Lenneberg (ed.), *New Directions in the Study of Language* (Cambridge, Mass.: MIT Press).

Ervin-Tripp, S. (1974), 'Is second language learning like the first?', *TESOL Quarterly*, vol. 8, no. 2, pp. 111–27.

Fanselow, J. (1977), 'Beyond Rashomon: conceptualising and describing the teaching act', *TESOL Quarterly*, vol. 11, no. 1, pp. 17–39.

Fathman, A. (1975), 'The relationship between age and second language productive ability', *Language Learning*, vol. 25, no. 2, pp. 245–54.

Fillmore, L.W. (1976), 'Individual differences in second language acquisition', paper presented to the Asilomar Conference on Individual Differences in Language Ability and Language Behaviour, Monterey, California.

Ferguson, C. A. (1964), 'Baby talk in six languages', *American Anthropologist*, vol. 66, pp. 103–14.

Fodor, J., Garrett, M. F., and Bever, T. G. (1974), *The Psychology of Language* (New York: McGraw Hill).

Fodor, J., and Garrett, M. (1966), 'Some reflections on competence and performance', in J. Lyons and R. Wales (eds), *Psycholinguistics Papers* (Edinburgh: Edinburgh University Press), pp. 135–82.

Frase, L. T. (1972), 'Maintenance and control in the acquisition of knowledge from written materials', in R. O. Freedle and J. B. Carroll (eds), *Language Comprehension and the Acquisition of Knowledge* (Washington, DC: Winston), pp. 337–60.

Fries, C. C. (1952), *The Structure of English* (New York: Harcourt Brace & World).

Fromkin, V. (ed.) (1973), *Speech Errors as Linguistic Evidence* (The Hague: Mouton).

Gage, N. L. (1963), 'Paradigms for research on teaching', in N. L. Gage (ed.), *Handbook of Research on Teaching* (Chicago: Rand McNally).

Gardner, R. C., and Lambert, W. E. (1959), 'Motivational variables in second language acquisition', *Canadian Journal of Psychology*, vol. 13, no. 4, pp. 266–72.

Gardner, R. C., and Lambert, W. E. (1972), *Attitudes and Motivation in Second Language Teaching* (Rowley, Mass.: Newbury House).

Gardner, R. C., and Smythe, P. C. (1975), 'Motivation and second language acquisition', *Canadian Modern Language Review*, vol. 31, pt 3, pp. 218–30.

Garrett, M. F., Bever, T. G., and Fodor, J. A. (1966), 'The active use of grammar in speech perception', *Perception and Psychophysics*, vol. 1, pp. 30–2.

Genesee, F. (1978), 'The role of intelligence in second language learning', *Language Learning*, vol. 26, no. 2, pp. 267–80.

Glaser, R. (1976), 'Components of a psychology of instruction: toward a science of design', *Review of Educational Research*, vol. 46, no. 1, pp. 1–24.

Good, T. L., and Brophy, J. E. (1978), *Looking in Classrooms* (New York: Harper & Row).

Goodman, Kenneth S. (1967), 'Reading: a psycholinguistic guessing game', *Journal of the Reading Specialist*, vol. 4, pp. 126–35; reprinted in D. V. Gunderson (ed.), *Language and Reading* (Washington, DC: Centre for Applied Linguistics).

Goodman, K. S. (1973), *Miscue Analysis* (Urbana, Ill.: University of Illinois Press).

Green, P. S. (ed.) (1975), *The Language Laboratory in School* (Edinburgh: Oliver & Boyd).

Guiora, A. Z., Paluszny, M., Beit-Hallahmi, B., Catford, J. C., Cooley, R. E., and Yoder Dull, C. (1975), 'Language and person – studies in language behaviour', *Language Learning*, vol. 25, pp. 43–61.

Hakuta, K. (1976), 'A case study of a Japanese child learning English as a second language', *Language Learning*, vol. 26, no. 2, pp. 321–51.

Halliday, M. A. K. (1970), 'Language structure and language function', in J. Lyons (ed.), *New Horizons in Linguistics* (Harmondsworth: Penguin).

Halliday, M. A. K. (1975), *Learning How to Mean* (London: Edward Arnold).

Hatch, E. M. (1974), 'Second language learning – universals?', *Working Papers in Bilingualism*, vol. 3, pp. 1–18.

Hatch, E. M. (1976), 'Discourse analysis, speech acts and second language acquisition', *Workpapers in TESL*, vol. 10, pp. 51–64.

Hatch, E. M. (ed.) (1978), *Second Language Acquisition* (Rowley, Mass.: Newbury House).

Hayhurst, H. (1967), 'Some errors of young children in producing passive sentences', *Journal of Verbal Learning and Verbal Behaviour*, vol. 6, pp. 634–39.

Miller, G. A., and McKean, K. O. (1964), 'A chronometric study of some relations between sentences', *Quarterly Journal of Experimental Psychology*, vol. 16, pp. 297–308.

Moody, K. (1976), 'A type of exercise for developing prediction skills in reading', *RELC Journal*, vol. 7, no. 1 (June) (Singapore).

Moulton, W. G. (1961), 'Linguistics and language teaching in the United States, 1940–1960', in C. Mohrmann, A. Sommerfelt and J. Whatmough (eds), *Trends in European & American Linguistics, 1930–1960* (Utrecht: Spectrum).

Mowrer, O. H. (1954), 'The psychologist looks at language', *The American Psychologist*, vol. 9, no. 11, pp. 660–94.

Naiman, N., Fröhlich, A., and Stern, H. (1975), *The Good Language Learner* (Modern Language Centre, Dept. of Curriculum, Ontario Institute for Studies in Education).

Nash, R. (1976), 'Pupils' expectations of their teachers', in M. Stubbs and S. Delamont (eds), *Explorations in Classroom Observation* (London: Wiley).

Neisser, U. (1967), *Cognitive Psychology* (New York: Appleton-Century-Crofts).

Nelson, K. (1973), 'Structure and strategy in learning to talk', *Monographs of the Society for Research in Child Development*, no. 149.

Neufeld, G. (1976), 'The bilingual's lexical store', *International Review of Applied Linguistics*, vol. 14, no. 1, pp. 15–31.

Ockenden, M. (1972), *Situational Dialogues* (London: Longman).

Oller, J., and Obrecht, D. (1969), 'The psycholinguistic principle of informational sequence: an experiment in second language learning', *International Review of Applied Linguistics*, vol. 7, pp. 117–23.

Osgood, C. E. (1963), 'On understanding and creating sentences', *American Psychologist*, vol. 18, pp. 735–51.

Osgood, C. E. (1971), 'Where do sentences come from?', in D. Steinberg and L. A. Jakobovits (eds), *Semantics, an Interdisciplinary Reader* (Cambridge: CUP).

Ott, C. E., Butler, D. C., Blake, R. S., and Ball, J. P. (1973), 'The effect of interactive-image elaboration on the acquisition of foreign language vocabulary', *Language Learning*, vol. 23, no. 2, pp. 197–206.

Pickett, G. D. (1978), *The Foreign Language Learning Process* (London: British Council English Teaching Information Centre).

Pimsleur, P. (1968a), *Language Aptitude Battery* (New York: Harcourt Brace & World).

Pimsleur, P. (1968b), 'Language aptitude testing', in A. Davies (ed.), *Language Testing Symposium* (London: OUP).

Pimsleur, P., Mosberg, L., and Morrison, A. L. (1962), 'Student factors in foreign language learning', *Modern Language Journal*, vol. 46, pp. 160–70.

Pimsleur, P., Sundland, D., and MacIntyre, R. D. (1964), 'Underachievement in foreign language learning', *International Review of Applied Linguistics*, vol. 2, no. 2, pp. 113–50.

Richards, J. C. (1971), 'A non-contrastive approach to error analysis', *English Language Teaching*, vol. 25, no. 3, pp. 204–19.

Rigg, P. (1976), 'Reading in ESL', in J. F. Fanselow and R. Crymes (eds), *On TESOL '76* (Washington DC: TESOL), pp. 203–10.

Rivers, W. (1964), *The Psychologist and the Foreign Language Teacher* (Chicago: University of Chicago Press).

Rivers, W. (1971), 'Linguistic and psychological factors in speech perception and their implications for teaching materials', in P. Pimsleur and T. Quinn (eds), *The Psychology of Second Language Learning* (Cambridge: CUP), pp. 123–34.

Robson, C. (1973), *Experiment, Design and Statistics in Psychology* (Harmondsworth: Penguin).

Rogers, J. (ed.) (1978), *Group Activities for Language Learning*, Occasional Paper No. 4 (Singapore: SEAMEO, RELC).

Rosansky, E. (1977), 'Methods and morphemes in second language acquisition research', *Language Learning*, vol. 26, no. 2, pp. 409–25.

Rosch, E. H. (née Heider) (1973), 'On the internal structure of perceptual and semantic categories', in T. E. Moore (ed.), *Cognitive Development and the Acquisition of Language* (New York: Academic Press).

Rothkopf, E. (1970), 'The concept of mathemagenis activities', *Review of Educational Research*, vol. 40, no. 3, pp. 325–36.

Rubin, J. (1975), 'What the "good language learner" can teach us', *TESOL Quarterly*, vol. 9, no. 1, pp. 41–51.

Rutherford, W. E. (1972), *Modern English*, 2nd ed. (Harcourt Brace Jovanovich).

Sachs, J. S. (1967), 'Recognition memory for syntactic and semantic aspects of connected discourse', *Perception and Psychophysics*, vol. 2, pp. 437–42.

Sarbin, T. R., and Jones, D. S. (1956), 'An experimental analysis of role behaviour', *Journal of Abnormal and Social Psychology*, vol. 51, pp. 236–41. Reprinted in E. E. Maccoby, T. M. Newcomb and E. L. Hartley (eds), *Readings in Social Psychology* (London: Methuen, 1958).

Savin, H. B., and Perchonock, E. (1965), 'Grammatical structure and immediate recall of sentences', *Journal of Verbal Learning and Verbal Behaviour*, vol. 4, pp. 348–53.

Schumann, J. H. (1976), 'Social distance as a factor in second language acquisition', *Language Learning*, vol. 26, no. 1, pp. 135–43.

Scollon, R. (1976), 'One child's language from one to two: the origins of construction', unpublished PhD dissertation, University of Hawaii.

Selinker, L. (1972), 'Interlanguage', *International Review of Applied Linguistics*, vol. 10, no. 3, pp. 201–31.

Sinclair, J., and Coulthard, M. (1975), *Towards an Analysis of Discourse* (London: OUP).

Sinclair de Zwart, H. (1973), 'Language acquisition and cognitive development', in T. Moore (ed.), *Cognitive Development and the Acquisition of Language* (New York: Academic Press).

Skinner, B. F. (1957), *Verbal Behaviour* (New York: Appleton-Century-Crofts).

Slobin, D. I. (1973), 'Cognitive prerequisites for the development of grammar', in C. A. Ferguson and D. I. Slobin (eds), *Studies of Child Language Development* (New York: Holt, Rinehart & Winston), pp. 183–6.

Sperry, L. (ed.) (1972), *Learning Performance and Individual Differences* (Glenview, Ill.: Scott, Foresman).

Spolsky, B. (1969), 'Attitudinal aspects of second language learning', *Language Learning*, vol. 19, no. 3, pt 4, pp. 271–85.

Stern, H. H. (1974), 'What can we learn from the good language learner?' *Canadian Modern Language Review*, vol. 31, pp. 304–18.

Stevick, E. (1971), 'Evaluating and adapting language materials', in H. Allen and R. Campbell (eds), *Teaching English as a Second Language*, 2nd ed. (New York: McGraw-Hill), pp. 102–7.

Stevick, E. (1976), *Memory Meaning and Method* (Rowley, Mass.: Newbury House).

Strevens, P. (1974), 'Theoretical studies of the language learning/teaching process', paper prepared at the Culture Learning Institute, East–West Center, Honolulu, Hawaii.

Stubbs, M. (1976), 'Keeping in touch: some functions of teacher talk', in M. Stubbs and S. Delamont (eds), *Explorations in Classroom Observation* (London: Wiley).

Sturtridge, G., McAlpin, J., and Harper, D. (1977), 'The British Council and the language problems of overseas students': English for academic purposes: materials development. Appendix 1a, 'Morts', in A. P. Cowie and J. B. Heaton (eds), *English for Academic Purposes* (Reading: British Association of Applied Linguistics/Specialised English Language Materials for Overseas University Students), p. 113.

Symposium on Individualised Instruction, *Modern Language Journal* (1975), vol. 59, no. 5 (November), pp. 323–66.

Taylor, I. (1971), 'How are words from two languages organised in bilinguals' memory?', *Canadian Journal of Psychology*, vol. 25, pp. 228–40.

Thelen, H. A. (1967), *Classroom Grouping for Teachability* (New York: Wiley).

Tongue, R. K., and others (1977), *Controlled and Guided Composition*, Occasional Paper No. 3 (Singapore: SEAMEO, RELC).

Tucker, G. R., Hamayan, E., and Genesee, F. H. (1976), 'Affective, cognitive and social factors in second language acquisition', *Canadian Modern Language Review*, vol. 32, no. 3, pp. 214–26.

Tulving, E. (1966), 'Subjective organisation and effects of repetition in multi-trial free-recall learning', *Journal of Verbal Learning and Verbal Behaviour*, vol. 5, pp. 193–7.

Tulving, E. (1972), 'Episodic and semantic memory', in E. Tulving and W. Donaldson (eds), *Organisation of Memory* (New York: Academic Press).

Tulving, E., and Pearlstone, Z. (1966), 'Availability versus accessibility of information in memory for words', *Journal of Verbal Learning and Verbal Behaviour*, vol. 5, pp. 381–91.

Upshur, J. (1968), 'Four experiments on the relation between foreign language teaching and learning', *Language Learning*, vol. 21, pp. 197–204.

Vernon, M. D. (1969), *Human Motivation* (Cambridge: CUP).

Von Wright, J. M. (1957), 'An experimental study of human serial learning', *Societa Scientia Fenmica Commentationes Humanorum Litterarum*.

Vygotsky, L. S. (1962), *Thought and Language* (Cambridge, Mass.: MIT Press/ Wiley).

Wagner-Gough, J. (1975), 'Comparative studies in second language learning', *CAL-ERIC/CLL Series on Language and Linguistics*, no. 26 (June); reprinted in Hatch (1978), pp. 155–71.

Wason, P. C. (1964), 'On the failure to eliminate hypotheses – a second look', in P. C. Wason and P. N. Johnson-Laird (eds), *Thinking and Reasoning* (Harmondsworth: Penguin).

Wason, P. C. (1965), 'The contexts of plausible denial', *Journal of Verbal Learning and Verbal Behaviour*, vol. 4, pp. 7–11.

Watcyn-Jones, P. (1978), *Act English* (Harmondsworth: Penguin).

Weiner, B. (1972a), *Theories of Motivation: From Mechanism to Cognition* (Chicago: Markham).

Weiner, B. (1972b), 'Attribution theory, achievement motivation, and the educational process', *Review of Educational Research*, vol. 42, no. 2, pp. 203–15.

Weiner, B., and Kukla, A. (1970), 'An attributional analysis of achievement motivation', *Journal of Personality and Social Psychology*, vol. 15, pp. 1–20.

Welford, A. T. (1968), *Fundamentals of Skill* (London: Methuen).

Widdowson, H. G. (1978), *Teaching Language as Communication* (Oxford: OUP).

Wight, J. (1976), 'The normal classroom as a context for EL_2 learning', paper delivered to the British Association of Applied Linguistics seminar Languages for Life, Southampton, December.

Wilkins, D. (1972), *Linguistics in Language Teaching* (Leeds: E. J. Arnold).

Wilkins, D. (1976), *Notional Syllabuses* (London: Longman).

Wode, H. (1976), 'Developmental sequences in naturalistic L_2 acquisition', *Working Papers in Bilingualism*, vol. 11, pp. 1–31.

Woodworth, R. S., and Schlosberg, H. (1955), *Experimental Psychology* (London: Methuen).

Wragg, E. C. (1970), 'Interaction analysis in the foreign language classroom', *Modern Language Journal*, vol. 54, pp. 116–26.

Wright, J. M. von (1957), 'An experimental study of human serial learning', *Soc. Sci. Fenmica Commentationes Humanorum Litterarum*, vol. 23, no. 1.

Index